WHEELS ACROSS THE DESERT

Wheels Across the Desert

Exploration of the Libyan Desert by Motorcar 1916-1942

by
Andrew Goudie

Silphium Press

Wheels Across the Desert:
Exploration of the Libyan Desert by Motor Car 1916-1942
by Andrew Goudie

Produced by Silphium Books, an imprint of
The Society for Libyan Studies
c/o The Institute of Archaeology
31-34 Gordon Square, London WC1H 0PY
www.britac.ac.uk/institutes/libya

Cover illustration shows a Model T Ford of the Light Car Patrols from Nöther, 2003, *Die Erschliessung der Sahara durch Motorfahrzeuge 1901-1936*. Belleville, Munich, fig. 24.

ISBN 978-1-900971-07-2

Designed and typeset in TW Cent and Adobe Garamond Pro
by Primavera Quantrill
www.quantrillmedia.com

Printed by Lane's Printers, Broadstairs, Kent

Contents

Abbreviations

ADC	Aide-de-camp
ANZAC	Australia and New Zealand Army Corps (1914-18)
cc	cubic centimetres (engine capacity)
CMG	Companion (of the order) of St Michael and St George (an honour mostly awarded to diplomats)
Cwt	hundredweight (8 stones or 50.80 kg)
DSO	Distinguished Service Order (Military Decoration rewarding distinguished service in war)
GHQ	General Headquarters
HMS	His / Her Majesty's Ship
hp	horsepower
LRDG	Long Range Desert Group
LRP	Long Range Patrols, a short-lived name for what became known as the Long Range Desert Group (LRDG)
Lt	Lieutenant
Lt Col	Lieutenant Colonel
MC	Military Cross
NASA	National Aeronautics and Space Administration (USA)
OBE	Officer of the Order of the British Empire
POW	Prisoner of War
RAF	Royal Air Force
RGS	Royal Geographical Society
RFC	Royal Flying Corps
SAS	Special Air Service
VC	Victoria Cross (the highest military decoration awarded for valour 'in the face of the enemy' to members of the armed forces of some Commonwealth countries, and previous British Empire territories)

Preface

To some people deserts are repulsive, and it is often said that the Egyptian peasant living in the green fields of the Nile valley sees little point in venturing out into the bare wildernesses that lie on either side. However, like many others, I have always been fascinated by deserts. The motives that entice people to visit them are many. For some, like Moses and Elijah or Jesus and St John the Baptist, the motive has tended to be spiritual and religious. For others – engineers, water drillers, arms pedlars, oil men and drugs traffickers – the motives have been financial and material. For men like T.E. Lawrence and Wilfred Thesiger, both of whom spent time in the Western Desert, the attraction has been in part to find, understand and live with that sometimes elusive 'Noble Arab'. Certainly, Lawrence preferred Arab company to "the feral smell of English soldiers: that hot pissy aura of thronged men in woollen clothes". Others have gone to deserts to fight wars on behalf of their rulers, and that was true of the Western Desert in two world wars. Others go to deserts to seek out the remains of ancient cultures and civilizations or of past climates, for in a dry landscape these have often survived in a near-miraculous way. A few go to deserts for pure adventure, namely to attempt some spectacular first crossing of a sand sea with a spitting camel. For others, including one of the heroes of this book, Ralph Bagnold, it is the stark clarity and beauty of desert landscapes that is so mesmerizing. Still others go to deserts to undertake scientific study of desert phenomena. Our attempts to understand the environment of Mars have, not least in the Western Desert, become a major motive. The weather can also be an attraction at the right times of year, particularly on damp, dark, dank winter nights in the Thames floodplain.

I have, to varying degrees, been touched by all but one of these motives. I have also been lucky to visit Libya and Egypt on a variety of occasions over the last forty years and would particularly like to thank Professor Nabil Embabi, Professor Mahmoud Ashour, Dr Owais A. El-Rashidi,

S. Samieh, Dr. Stephen Stokes, Joseph Ballard, Amy Carter, Chris Pearson, James Cook, and my family, for their company in recent times. The late Professor Ronald Peel, always willing to talk with young colleagues, whetted my appetite for the theme of this book by recounting to me on one desert evening all the excitements he had enjoyed in the Gilf Kebir when working there in 1938 with Ralph Bagnold. I once met Ralph Bagnold himself fleetingly, when he was presented with an award by the British Geomorphological Research Group, but he remembered me and sent me a signed copy of a book he had produced with NASA on the similarities between the south-west of Egypt and the planet Mars. I treasure it.

I am also grateful to Professor Claudio Vita-Finzi and the Silphium Press for encouraging me to publish this book, and I hope that it will be of some modest benefit to the admirable Society for Libyan Studies. The book contains many photographs, nearly all of them old, and I am grateful to those who have so generously permitted me to reproduce them. However, in spite of my best efforts it has not been possible in all cases to make contact with the original photographers (most of whom are dead) or their publishers (many of whom are defunct) to seek copyright clearance. In all cases, however, I have listed the source from which I obtained them. Ailsa Allen of the Oxford University Centre for the Environment kindly drew the maps.

Andrew Goudie,
Oxford, October 2008

The desert is terrible and it is merciless,
but to the desert all those who once have known it must return

Hassanein Bey (1925, 29)

A DARING RAID

Deep in the desert of southern Libya, 450 km from the border with Algeria, lies the oasis of Murzuk. With its fort, small air-field, sand dunes and palms, it was the administrative centre of the southern Fezzan. Based there was an Italian garrison. Although at the end of 1940 the Second World War was already well advanced, the garrison must have felt relatively safe and sleepy, for it was isolated and distant from any British attack, protected by the depths of the desert in which it lay.

Far to the south of Murzuk lay the French province of Chad. After the fall of France in June 1940, most French overseas possessions were loyal to the pro-German Vichy government, but the position of Chad was more uncertain. A British army officer, Ralph Bagnold, was flown from Khartoum to Fort Lamy, the capital of Chad, to assess the situation. There he met the Governor, a modest, cultured and immensely talented black African from French Guiana, called Félix Sylvestre Eboué, whom Bagnold called "the shrewd little negro" (figure 1). With him was a fine, swaggering, tall, fair-haired Corsican Lieutenant Colonel with a monocle, Jean Colonna D'Ornano, the army second in command. Both of them were sympathetic to de Gaulle's Free French and under Eboué's leadership Chad became the first French colony to reject the Nazis' puppet Vichy regime in France and Marshal Pétain, its head of State. A deal was done. It was arranged that some Commonwealth forces, under Major Pat Clayton and Captain Michael Crichton Stuart, would drive across from Cairo, rendezvous with D'Ornano and his troops, and attack the Italian garrison in Murzuk.

Put like that it sounds easy, but to reach their destination, the British had to drive well over 2,000 km across the world's largest tract of extreme desert in small Chevrolet trucks with only rear-wheel drive. Moreover, they had to cross the enormous dunes of the Great Sand Sea that lies on the western borders of Egypt.

Figure 1. Félix Eboué, "the shrewd little negro" with de Gaulle in Chad.

Figure 2. Major Clayton (second from right) with Lt Col J.C. d'Ornano (second from left) just before the Murzuk Raid.

Clayton's force consisted of two patrols, termed 'G' and 'T' patrols, of what became the Long Range Desert Group (LRDG), one of them composed of New Zealanders (T) and the other of Guards (G). A full account of the raid is given by the leader of G Patrol, Captain Crichton Stuart. There were 76 men in 26 vehicles. They left Cairo on Boxing Day 1940, and eighteen days later, on 11 January 1941, having joined up with the French (figure 2), an event that was celebrated with Pernod, they attacked Murzuk in broad daylight, to the total surprise of the Italians. The airfield was destroyed, thick black smoke arose from the burning hangar and the noise of exploding bombs was heard for a long time. The enemy made no attempt at pursuit, and as they drove away the victorious patrols were concealed providentially in a dust storm which blew down from the north.

The raid was a daring and devastating success (Bimberg 2002), though D'Ornano was killed in a burst of machine gun from behind a hangar at the airfield. One New Zealander, Sergeant C.D. Hewson, was also killed when he stood up to repair his jammed machine gun. The raid had a most alarming effect on Italian morale across Libya. From that time on, no garrison and no convoy of vehicles would ever be absolutely secure. Just how had Clayton's small force managed to conquer not only the Italians but also the immensity of the Libyan Desert?

Immensity

The Nile, a green, snaking line of fertility, slices through Egypt (figures 3 & 4). The world's longest river, its water and its silt, derived some thousands of kilometres away in eastern and central Africa, supports one of the oldest and most closely packed agricultural populations in the world. Without it, neither the great civilisations of the past nor the teeming, vividly green fields and brown mud-brick villages of the present would exist. Rudyard Kipling went so far as to describe Egypt as not a country but "a longish strip of market garden". Egypt is veritably the gift of the Nile. To its east is the Eastern Desert, the mountainous tract through which tourists pass en route from the temples of Luxor and Karnak to the diving resorts on the Red Sea. To its west is the Western or Libyan Desert, the eastern part of the great Sahara, the world's largest tract of aridity. From the Nile to the Atlantic, a distance of 4,800 km, all is desert. Its dunes, salt flats, gravel plains and occasional mountains contrast with the startling green of the Nile Valley. The huge, vibrant and noisy cities, of which Cairo is the ultimate example, are the antithesis of the solitude and emptiness of the deserts on either side. Michael Mason, who travelled the Libyan Desert in the 1930s, summed up its character in this way:

> The Libyan Desert lies immense and idle, scorching and stewing in the dancing mirage of noon; pale and ghostly beneath the cold moon of night; vast as India; sterile and barren as India is teeming with life; the skeleton of a great land dead of drought, crumbling beneath the sand-blast. When men's souls yearn for the peace of a great emptiness they turn to the deserts, the snowfields or the sea. Earth's greatest spaces of utter emptiness are Antarctica, the interior of Greenland and the Libyan Desert. (Mason 1936, 13).

The Libyan Desert is not the driest place on earth. That is a record that is held by the Atacama Desert in Chile. The Atacama is relatively small and

Figure 3. The Nile Valley near the Valley of the Kings, Luxor.

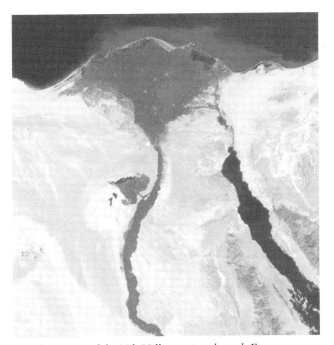

Figure 4. Satellite image of the Nile Valley passing through Egypt.

17

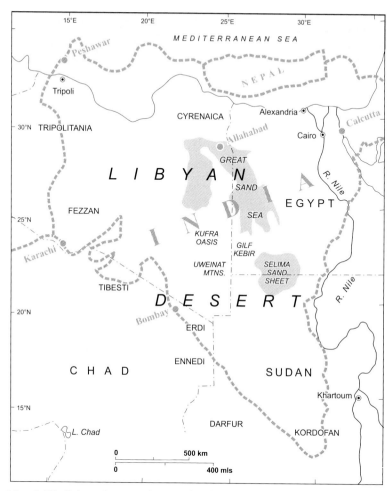

Map 1. The Libyan Desert – the size of India.

narrow, squeezed between the snow-capped Andes and the cold waters of the Pacific Ocean. The Libyan Desert, by contrast, is a huge stretch of territory that extends hundreds of kilometres from the Mediterranean to the Sudan and from the Nile to the mountains of the Central Sahara. In shape and extent it resembles the Indian Peninsula (map 1). Though not as dry as the

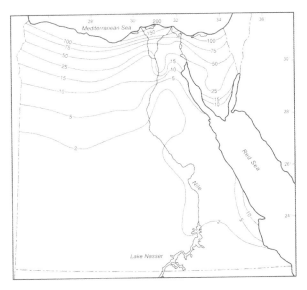

Map 2. The Rainfall of Egypt (mm).

Atacama, it is still incredibly arid and parched. Rainfall decreases progressively as one moves southwards from the Mediterranean coast (map 2). At its centre, the mean annual rainfall is no more than 1 mm and rain may not fall for years on end. Death Valley in California has over 60 times as much rain. It is no wonder that mummified bodies from sites some thousands of years old have never rotted, still possessing their skin, hair, and fingernails. It is no wonder that sardine cans left by British soldiers in the First World War have never rusted. Less prosaically, the desert's aridity has preserved a wonderful assortment of archaeological treasures. As Rudolph Kuper (2002, 1) put it, "The desert keeps it all: their remains and ours, as well as the evidence of millennia of earlier human activities, which is omnipresent". On the other hand, occasional rain-storms do occur. When Gerhard Rohlfs, the German explorer, was west of Dakhla in 1874 he experienced a downpour, restocked and watered his camels, and left a cairn at the place he had named Regenfeld. Similarly, when

C.S. Jarvis, a colonial administrator, first arrived in Kharga oasis, he was told that there had not been a shower for 25 years. Thus when 30 tonnes of cement arrived to start new buildings, Jarvis said there was no need to cover them up as there hadn't been rain there in the lifetime of man. That same night there was a cloudburst and thirty tons of cement set into solid blocks in its sacks.

The Libyan Desert has not always been dry. Radar images from the Space Shuttle revealed the presence of ancient drainage systems – 'radar rivers' – filled with alluvium and now often covered by a veneer of wind-blown sand. The Wadi Howar, a defunct tributary of the Nile, was once a huge system, teeming with hippopotamus, crocodiles and toads. Large fans of alluvium have been mapped to the east of the Gilf Kebir (Robinson *et al.* 2007). In addition, large freshwater lakes have been found at places like Nabta Playa and Oyo, and pollen analysis of their sediments has revealed that what is now bare desert was formerly savannah. In the Sudan the 'Northern Darfur Megalake' may have covered 30,750 km^2, while in Libya a massive water body, to which the name 'Lake Megafezzan' has been given, covered some 159,000 km^2. Another even larger lake, called 'Mega-Chad' covered over 400,000 km^2 of the area now occupied by Lake Chad and the Bodélé depression, stretching northwards close to the mountains of Tibesti and Ennedi. Radiocarbon dates suggest that such lakes were in existence as recently as 9,000-6,000 years ago. There are also great spreads of freshwater carbonates, called tufa, which were deposited by springs and streams and now drape places like the precipitous cliffs overlooking Kharga. Beautiful stone tools are often found associated with the tufas, indicating that these areas were attractive sites for settlement. The tufas, now often blackened by millennia of desert weathering, contain the encrusted and fossilised remains of fig trees (*Ficus*), palms and ferns. In addition, large mounds – spring mounds – mark points where groundwater used to flow more copiously than today. Water from spring mounds was used for irrigation in prehistoric and historic times, and the damp, vegetated, irrigated areas trapped wind-blown sand, causing the land surface to build up. There are also remarkable amounts of rock art at Uweinat and elsewhere with depictions of big mammals such as giraffe, while spread across the barren desert surface there are extensive scatters of stone tools, cattle-tethering stones, fire-places, and the like, that show that the Libyan desert was extensively inhabited in former wet phases. For example, people moved into the Libyan Desert around 12,000 years ago when monsoonal rains produced a savannah-like environment. Between 9,000 and 7,300 years ago domestic stock were introduced and settlement became well established all over the area (Bubenzer and Riemer, 2007). Scientists talk about 'The African Humid Period' and the 'Greening of the Sahara'. After around 5,500 years ago, rainfall became less reliable and plentiful, and there was a marked retreat of humans from extensive tracts of what had now become harsh desert (Kuper 2006; Kindermann *et al.* 2006). Today's desert ecosystem, dust storms and winds were established by about 2,700 years ago (Kröpelin *et al.* 2008).

This book is the story of how intrepid groups of British, European and Egyptian explorers, both military and civilian, seized the opportunity provided by the development of the motor car to travel, map and understand the previously largely trackless wastes of the world's most forbidding desert. They travelled through what the greatest of all the desert explorers, Ralph Bagnold, called 'Immensity' (1935, 12). They were attracted by what Prince Kemal el Din Hussein later called "A veritable pole of repulsion or rather, a dead region of the globe". It is a story every bit as intriguing as the better-known histories of the search for the sources of the Nile or of the race to the Poles.

THE LIBYAN (WESTERN) DESERT

The Libyan Desert is not, in terms of scenic diversity perhaps, the most alluring of the world's great deserts. It does not, for example, have the great backdrop of snow-capped volcanic mountains that makes the Atacama so special. Neither does it have enormous canyons and mountains like some of the deserts of North America. For the most part the Libyan Desert is rather flat and only limited areas reach altitudes greater than a few hundred metres above sea level (map 3). The Egyptian geomorphologist, Professor Nabil Embabi, has written a wonderful summary of our knowledge of its landscapes. Much of it is underlain by relatively gently-dipping limestone, shale and sandstone strata of Cretaceous to Miocene age that create low escarpments and gently sloping plateaux. The Libyan Desert Plateau (El Diffa) in the north of the region was described by G.W. Murray (1967, 168), as "a ham-shaped country of nothing at all – no mountains, not even hills – no rivers, not even wadis – no oases, no springs – just nothing but nothing and plenty of that." One intriguing type of surface, developed on Lower Eocene rocks, is called *El Botikh* – the water melons. This is formed by the weathering out of large, globular concretions, which may be so thickly strewn over the surface as to obstruct travel.

High land tends only to occur in the south-west of the region in the Gilf Kebir, a huge erosional remnant of sandstone attaining heights of more than 1,000 m above sea-level, and at the crystalline Gebel Uweinat which rises to over 1,900 m.

The Gilf Kebir (figure 5) roughly equals Switzerland in size, and its south-eastern part has sheer cliffs. These forbidding barriers have an approximate total frontage of 3,000 km. Crossed by the Tropic of Cancer it consists of two plateaux that are connected by a narrow bridge. The south-eastern plateau is on its own about the size of Corsica. The Gilf is serrated by a series of large, canyon-like wadis (Lingstädter and Kröpelin 2004).

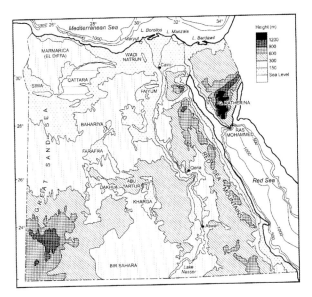

Map 3. The Relief of Egypt.

Gebel Uweinat, the highest point in the Libyan Desert, and the neighbouring massifs of Arkenu and Kissu, are mostly granitic mountains that formed before the sandstones surrounding them. However, the eastern part of Uweinat consists of a large block of Palaeozoic sandstone, resting upon Precambrian basement rocks. In prehistoric times, the valleys (*karkurs*) that cut into Uweinat, were densely populated, as attested by the hundreds of rock paintings and engravings that may be found in rock shelters along their sides. 'Uweinat' means 'the little springs', and its name reflects its importance as a storm-fed water point isolated on all sides by barren, "howling" desert (Shaw 1934, 63). South-western Egypt also possesses the world's largest spread of craters, though whether they are caused by meteorite impact or are hydrothermal vents is still a matter of debate. More than 1,300 of them have been detected to the east of the Gilf Kebir.

The desert also has some major low-lying depressions, often bounded by steep cliffs, which have been excavated in part by millennia of wind

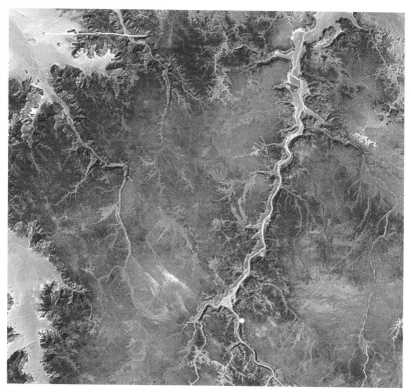

Figure 5. A satellite image of the western part of the Gilf Kebir Plateau. Scale bar is 5 km.

erosion. This has also moulded the ground into aerodynamically shaped landforms called yardangs or mud lions, named thus because of their supposed resemblance in shape to those reclining carnivores (figure 6). The depressions – Fayum, Qattara, Farafra, Bahariya, Dakhla, Kurkur, Kharga, and Siwa – are places where underground groundwater reservoirs approach the ground surface and allow oases of date palms to occur. This underground water is present in the Nubian Sandstone (Palaeozoic to Cretaceous) aquifer, which consists of a thickness of up to 3,500 m of sands, sandstones and other porous sedimentary rocks. This artesian system is of huge extent, covering some 2.5 million km². The subterranean water

Figure 6a. Bahariya yardangs – wind-fluted terrain.

Figure 6b. Wind-moulded chalk in the White Desert of Farafra.

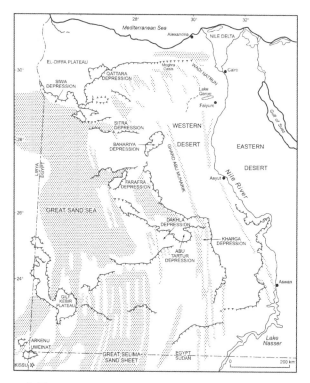

Map 4. Dune fields in Egypt.

moves over 1,000 km in a north-easterly direction from recharge areas in the mountains of northern Chad. Much of the water is of considerable antiquity, some as much as a million years old, and is a fossil resource that was probably created by past humid periods. It is now being heavily exploited so that the water table is dropping in some of the oases. This is the case in Kufra, where water is being transported away to Tripoli, Sirte and Benghazi in the great 4 m diameter pre-stressed concrete pipes of the 'Great Man-made River Project'.

Some of the depressions are excavated below sea level, most notably Qattara, the base of which lies at 133 m lower than the surface of the Mediterranean, Fayum, which lies at -45 m, and Siwa which lies at -25 m.

Figure 7. Satellite image of linear dune chains of the Great Sand Sea. Scale: 5 km.

During wetter intervals of the past some of the depressions contained large lakes and even now some of them are damp, so that vehicles that attempt to cross them can easily get bogged down in expanses of treacherous, saline clays. The depressions may have been initiated by ancient river systems that flowed towards the retreating Tethys Ocean during the Tertiary period, cutting down into the various layers of sedimentary rock. Limestone layers may have been dissolved away during past wet phases. However, in whatever way they were initiated, they have subsequently been enlarged by wind, acting in concert with aggressive salts that broke up the underlying rocks into fine materials that could easily be blown away.

Elsewhere the desert winds have moulded sand into fields of dunes – sand seas or *ergs* (map 4). The greatest of these is appropriately called the Great Sand Sea (figure 7). Beginning just south of Siwa oasis, it continues almost uninterrupted for 600 km to the Gilf Kebir plateau, and covers some 150,000 km^2 of eastern Libya and western Egypt. Most of the dunes are great ridges, called whale-backs, upon which long, parallel ridges called *seifs*, run more or less north to south in response to the trend of the dominant

Figure 8a. Crescentic barchan dunes in the Kharga Oasis, Egypt (seen from the ground).

Figure 8b. Crescentic barchan dunes in the Kharga Oasis, Egypt (satellite image). Scale: 1 km.

winds. Ralph Bagnold described them as being "like notched caterpillars end to end in continuous chains" (1935, 149). Some of these dunes are immensely long, and in the 1930s the Hungarian scientist Ladislas Kádár traced one that was 140 km long from end to end. Because of their height, width (often 1 km or more), steepness and instability, they pose a formidable barrier to travel from east to west, from Egypt to Libya, for a large proportion of the dune summits attain heights of more than 100 m above the underlying plains. The general direction of the whale-backs is approximately south-south-east, which reflects the persistence of winds from the north north-west or north. As Major Jarvis remarked:

Those people who have come on deck in a mail steamer during a gale in the Atlantic and have looked across the grey and white waste of huge waves will recall the feeling of awe they experienced at seeing the ocean in one of its uncontrollable moods.…This is precisely the feeling one has when one stands for the first time on an outlying dune in the Siwa sand sea, and looks out across huge billows a hundred to two hundred feet in height, which roll on apparently increasing in size until they fade into the haze of the horizon. One feels that to venture into the menacing waste in a small car is to court death, and as a matter of fact this is a fairly sound appreciation, as, if anything happens to the car or one should lose one's way, death from thirst or starvation is inevitable. (Jarvis 1943, 142).

Others dunes are mobile little crescentic bodies, called barchans (figure 8), which travel at rates of around 10 m per year and often overwhelm roads, tracks, railways and settlements. Their horns point in the direction of their movement, and on their lee sides they have a steep slope down which sand avalanches. Huge numbers of them, derived from the Abu Moharik sand-belt to the north, plunge over the limestone escarpment that bounds the northern part of the Kharga depression, and then march relentlessly southwards in their hundreds across the depression's floor. In the 1980s, the American archaeologist, C. Vance Haynes was able to resurvey a 20 m-high barchan

Figure 9. A satellite image of a large dust storm blowing off the Libyan Desert into the Mediterranean.

that had first been surveyed by Ralph Bagnold in 1930, and found that over a 57-year period it had moved at about 7.5 m per year.

Other types of dune build up either against or in the lee of topographic barriers. Kádár (1934, 475) termed them 'sand-dams' or 'tail-dunes' respectively. He found one against the north-east rampart of the Gilf Kebir that was 126 m high. Some of these features can prove to be an obstacle while others, if in the right situation, banked up against a cliff, provide a ramp up onto a plateau surface which would otherwise be too steep to be scalable.

The dune sands and other parts of the desert surface can be whipped up into dust storms and sandstorms locally called *khamsin* or *haboob* (figure 9). Dust storms are defined as events where the presence of large amount of talc-sized silt in the air causes visibility to be reduced to less than 1,000 m. Strong frontal systems or convective storms scour and lift fine particles, unbound in the dry environment by either vegetation or moisture, into the air, and then can transport them over hundreds or even thousands of kilometres. They can also extend high into the atmosphere, creating problems for pilots. Sand storms are composed of coarser, more gritty material which travels along much closer to the ground surface. Both dust storms and sand storms pose problems for travellers, though some people have seen them as dramatic and beautiful. In the First World War, a leader of the Light Car Patrols, Claud Williams, described them as "the last word in beastliness" as they stopped drivers from seeing holes, bumps or constrictions, and blotted out the sun, which was a vital aid for direction finding. In January 1941, *The Times'* Special Correspondent wrote a particularly graphic account from Gazala in northern Libya:

A sandstorm of such blind fury has broken over Libya that the war is temporarily stopped. All yesterday it gathered until last night it burst with hurricane force, uprooting telegraph poles, sweeping lorries off roads, toppling tents, and blocking visibility down to five yards over the desert....

No plane can take the lemon-coloured air that seems to shriek past in whirlpools from every direction....Arabs roaming over the battlefield have flung themselves down among their blown robes to mumble their prayers for release from the storm.

I tried from the outset in an Army truck an hour after dawn to find my way to our rear positions; but I was forced back. Troops beside the way had clapped gas-masks to their faces in an attempt to get a clean breath of air into their lungs; but the sand is fast laying a deep coating over everything – men, animals, tents, trucks, and especially, it seems, over these cold sausages I am trying to eat. (*The Times,* 18 January 1941).

In the summer of the same year, Titch Cave, a member of an LRDG Patrol that had just come in from the desert, witnessed a dust storm at Siwa oasis, just as he and his colleagues were to sit down and have a rare meal, not of cold, sandy sausages, but of fresh meat:

The mutton was carefully cooked, while we all waited in anticipation, and after being carved was just about ready to be served when an excited voice from outside shouted, "— me! Come and look at this."

We all dashed out not knowing what quite to expect and there, all across the northern horizon, was a huge rolling cloud which must have been over 100 feet high. We watched in awe, our dinner forgotten, as the cloud rolled down over the northern cliffs and advanced towards us across the oasis....

It was the father and mother of a sandstorm which was beyond the experience of even the oldest members of our patrol. Of course, our dinner was ruined....(Morgan 2000, 85).

A New Zealand trooper, Frank Jopling, also in the LRDG, described a dust storm in Siwa in 1942:

We could see what looked like thick clouds of smoke pushing through each other in the cloud. And after a while again some of the nearer hills vanished in the cloud. But the best sight of all was as it came across the oasis. It looked as though an enormous dam had broken through and was crashing down on us. As it came across the palms and over the hill of ruins we could hear the wind, and just before it came upon us, the wind got up....Everything went dark and a dull orange colour and we couldn't see more than ten yards ahead of us. Sand and dust got everywhere, but in spite of the discomfort it as a sight I would very much like to see again. (O'Carroll 2002, 167).

Field Marshal Rommel also wrote graphically about a storm, locally called the *ghibli*, which took place in Libya in March 1941 while he was flying across the desert:

> ...we ran into sandstorms near Taourga, whereat the pilot, ignoring my abuse and attempts to get him to fly on, turned back, compelling me to continue the journey by car from the airfield at Misurata. Now we realised what little idea we had of the tremendous force of such a storm. Immense clouds of reddish dust obscured all visibility and forced the car's speed down to a crawl. Often the wind was so strong that it was impossible to drive along the Via Balbia. Sand streamed down the windscreen like water. We gasped in breath painfully through handkerchiefs held over our faces and sweat poured off our bodies in the unbearable heat. So this was the Ghibli. Silently I breathed my apologies to the pilot. A Luftwaffe officer crashed in a sandstorm that day. (Hart 1953, 105).

During the defence of Tobruk, an Australian, Bob Sykes, described another storm:

> The sandstorm came at us like an express train at about 40 mph with increasing gusts of wind. All the oxygen seemed to go out of the air, and the flies were maddening and swarming...I sat down in my dugout and waited, thinking it would be over in a few minutes, but suddenly I nearly panicked – the sand was coming through every crack. I thought I would be buried. I fought my way out. I could hardly stand up in the wind. The sand was whipping the skin off my face and hands. (Gilbert 1992, 31).

Dust and sand storms (figure 10) were not only uncomfortable for the humans who were forced to endure them. They could also be damaging to their vehicles and armaments as well. This was well described by one of the soldiers in Popski's Private Army, a special unit that operated behind enemy lines in the Second World War. As Park Yunnie wrote:

Figure 10. Dust storm over Khartoum in the 1930s.

It hit us like a whip-lash, taking our breath, leaving us cowed and defenceless, whimpering with pain. We couldn't breathe. Hot, smarting dust clogged our nostrils, seared the backs of our throats, coated our tongue and gritted in our teeth; drifts of fine-blown sand formed in the folds of our clothing, blew into our pockets and found its way through to our skins; sand piled up in the trucks, forming miniature dunes, stuck to the oily and greasy parts of the chassis, blew under the bonnet and sifted into the carburettor, the magneto, the unsealed working parts; grating sand filtered into the Vickers guns, jamming the ammunition pans; sand found its way into everything, everywhere. (Yunnie 2002, 20).

The side of his truck was polished like a mirror, every vestige of paint sanded off.

Elsewhere the wind has acted like a sand blaster, chiselling bare rock outcrops into a choppy terrain of angular, razor-sharp ridges and furrows. Called *kharafish*, these are one of the most difficult terrain types to cross and can cause havoc to car tyres and suspensions. The wind-fluted bedrock and sediment outcrops are called *yardangs,* a Turkmen word that was introduced by the great Swedish explorer and archaeologist, Sven Hedin, who encountered similar features on his travels in Central Asia in the early twentieth century.

Where rock outcrops have not been scoured by the wind, they have often become covered over the millennia in a dark, sometimes shiny, patina, called 'desert varnish'. This is generally only wafer thin, but when it is breached or scraped off, the lighter colour of the underlying rock becomes obvious. Inhabitants of the desert used this characteristic to produce some of the rock art – petroglyphs – that are found very widely. The patina is composed of the oxides of iron and manganese, but scientists have agonised over whether the crust is derived from chemicals created by the weathering of the rock itself, whether algae play a role, or whether some of it is formed from dust that has been deposited on the rock surface (Dietzel *et al.* 2008).

Although much of what has been said so far has perhaps given the impression that the Libyan Desert was a truly dreadful place in which to drive, this is not entirely true. As Sir Bernard Fergusson remarked in a politically incorrect introduction to Crichton Stuart's *G Patrol*:

> Obstacles there were; but for the most part it offered excellent going. With no rivers or lakes, no towns or forests, no mud, no cultivation (dare one add, no lady drivers?) most of the ordinary hazards of overland transport were absent. Desert features were quickly recognised as standard, to be surmounted when the right drill was applied. Escarpments seldom proved completely impassable; sand dunes succumbed to experience, equipment, technique and confidence. Dry wadis, which abounded, were at first looked at askance; they came to be welcomed as afforders of shade and cover. (Crichton Stuart 1958, 17).

One desert type that provides particularly good going is the desert pavement or stone pavement (figure 11). This consists of a

Figure 11. A desert pavement in Bahariya.

relatively smooth surface composed of a thin layer of gravel particles that has been created when the fine particles that were originally present in the host sediment were carried away by the wind, to leave a lag or armour of materials that were too large to be removed by this mechanism.

In the 1980s, NASA scientists used the Libyan Desert as an analogue for understanding the landscapes of Mars that were being revealed for the first time by various space probes. Mars is very dry, but may formerly have been well watered, so that there are traces of river systems that may in part have been fashioned by seepage of groundwater. Mars has violent, planet-embracing dust storms, great expanses of yardangs, and major sand seas. It also has large tracts of terrain surfaced by disintegrated volcanic rock, and some of the rock disintegration may have been achieved by aggressive salts. In all these respects, Mars and the Libyan Desert are remarkably similar.

In the winter months the climate of the desert is cool and nights can be very cold. This has been the favoured season for travel. In the summer air temperatures regularly exceed 40-50° C. The highest air temperature ever recorded on Earth was at El Azizia, south of Tripoli in Libya. On 13 September 1922, the thermometer reached 58° C. The ground surface can get even hotter. Zoologists working at Wadi Halfa, down at the Egypt-Sudan border, have recorded soil and sand temperatures that exceeded

80º C. Under such conditions survival becomes a problem, especially if water is in short supply. As the geologist Kenneth Sandford remarked:

> In the intense heat of summer, troops, even natives of the country, are liable to numerous infections and ailments which are reduced to vanishing point in winter....Machines also feel the heat: exposed metal gets too hot to touch with bare hands, engines overheat, and water-cooled systems boil....Rubber tyres also feel the heat, and wear and tear in many ways is enormously greater in summer than in winter not only on machines but on crews. (Sandford 1940, 380).

Of course, given the aridity of the area, water often *is* in short supply. Wells, springs and oases can be hundreds of kilometres apart. Car travel reduced the tyranny of water to a large extent, but it is noticeable how many of the journeys had to involve places like Uweinat, Selima and Ain Dalla, where a supply was assured. Even then water was in short supply and sometimes scarcer than petrol. On 4.5 litres of water per day for all purposes, it became something of an art to wash, shave, clean your teeth, and wash you feet, all in a mug of water, with the resultant glutinous fluid being strained and poured into the radiator of one's vehicle. Some desert travellers planned to wash a third of their bodies each day, for the sand whipped up by sandstorms and by the vehicles themselves became matted on the hairy parts of the body, and they felt the imperative need to wash it away, even though a fresh lot of sand was picked up almost at once.

Early travellers found the Sahara repellent, as this extract from Mary Somerville's *Physical Geography* plainly shows:

> The desert is alternately scorched by heat and pinched by cold. The wind blows from the east nine months in the year; and at the equinoxes it rushes in a hurricane, driving the sand in clouds before it, producing the darkness of night at midday, and overwhelming caravans of men and animals in common destruction. (Somerville 1858, 92).

Figure 12. A Roman fort in the Kharga Oasis.

The French Geographer, Elisée Reclus gave a sense of even deeper despair:

>...even the flea itself will not venture into these dreadful regions. The intense radiation of the enormous white or red surface of the desert dazzles the eyes; in this blinding light every object appears to be clothed with a sombre and preternatural tint. Occasionally, the traveller, when sitting upon his camel, is seized with the *râgle*, a kind of brain-fever, which causes him to see the most fantastical objects in his delirious dreams. Even those who retain the entire possession of their faculties and clearness of their vision, are beset by distant mirages....When the wind blows hard, the traveller's body is beaten by grains of sand, which penetrate even through his clothes and prick like needles. (Reclus 1871, 94-95).

Flies could be a pestilence, and some of the Desert Rats of the Second World War found that trying to kill them was like mopping up the

Mediterranean with a piece of blotting paper. They swarmed over food, and some of the British soldiers resignedly referred to them as the meat in their rations.

Quite a large number of the desert motorists used portions of one of the great trans-desert caravan routes of North Africa – the Darb el Arba'in. There are five such routes: from Morocco to Timbuktu, from Tunis via Aïr to Kano, from Tripoli via Murzuk to Lake Chad, from Benghazi via Kufra to Wadai, and the Darb el Arba'in. This runs from Assiut on the Nile, via Kharga, Selima, and Bir Natrun to Darfur in the northern Sudan. It was a route along which camel caravans transported slaves and precious commodities, and the bones of beasts and humans, overcome by the desert, marked its alignment. In all it is some 1,800 km long (Shaw 1929) and its Arabic name means 'the 40 days' road', though it had for long been in use before the Arabs gave it this name. The Pharaohs erected temples along it, and the Romans built fortresses to guard it (figure 12). However, it is far from certain that the journey was accomplished in forty days. As Michael Asher, who himself travelled parts of the route by camel, put it:

> It is likely that the title 'Forty Days' Road' referred only to the actual marching time, which might have been divided up into forty equal stretches of a little less than thirty miles each, the average daily marching distance of a camel. (Asher 1984, 56).

The south to north caravans with their large contingents of slaves would almost certainly have taken longer. G.W. Murray (1967, 149), however, believed that the '40' are the 'Companions of the Prophet' who, at some period of their legendary existence, must have visited the Sudan by this route.

Some of the caravans that traversed the road were colossal. W.G. Browne, who went along the route in 1796, and whose journey lasted longer than the prescribed 40 days, described a caravan of 2,000 camels and

1,000 slaves. Among the goods that were carried northwards were rhinoceros horns, hippopotamus teeth, ostrich feathers, gum arabic, spices, tamarinds, copper, peacocks, parrots and monkeys.

Count Almásy, the Austro-Hungarian aristocrat, soldier and explorer, who used the road in the 1930s, was greatly struck by the Darb el Arba'in and the evidence it provided of human and bestial misery:

The first that catches one's eye is not the endless snaking caravan trails, but the series of white patches that trail the bed of the caravan road.

Skeletons!

Hundreds and hundreds of sun whitened heaps of bones, in places densely by each other, then only sporadically, but continuously along the troughs of the Darb el Arba'in as far as the eye can see. They are mainly camel bones, some very ancient, half-covered by sand and fragmented, others complete, as if they were laid down for an anatomical study. No human bones are visible, but here and there a pile of stones covering a grave mark the forty days' road....some skeletons lie with the head arced back to the backbone, others with outstretched neck – The ones with the head curved back have been slaughtered....The camel herders cut the throat of the animals according to the law of the religion, that is why the necks are curved back. Such a skeleton indicates that the men were forced to drink the water carried in the stomach of the animal. (Almásy 1934, 21).

Llewellyn Beadnell, a geologist and hydrologist who from the 1890s carried out surveys of the desert oases, also noted the evidence for the demise of camels (Beadnell 1909, 34).

...on the Derb el Arbaîn, between Kharga and Assiut, the skeletons of these poor beasts are met with in groups of tens and twenties, and must number hundreds and thousands. In many instances the skeleton still lies undisturbed, in the position assumed by the luckless animal in its death agony, the long neck curved back by muscular contraction so that the skull lies in contact with the spine. When one sees these remains, half buried in the sand, the bones bleached snow-white by a pitiless sun, with still adhering fragments of skin and muscle dried hard as adamant, one cannot but feel pity for those patient 'ships of the desert,' wrecked almost within sight of port. (Beadnell 1909, 34).

He also reported the comments of the French explorer, Frédéric Caillaud, who in 1817 observed the arrival at Assiut of a caravan from Darfur that consisted of the staggering total of 16,000 individuals, of whom 6,000 were slaves – men, women and children:

They had been two months travelling in the deserts, in the most intense heat of the year; meagre, exhausted, and the aspect of death on their countenances, the spectacle strongly excited compassion.

G.W. Murray was also struck by the piles of bones:

From Sheb we ran northwards along the Arba'in itself, truly "a way to death", for every twenty paces or so we came to a heap of bones where some strong camel had died of thirst or exhaustion. That was on the flat ground, at every little rise the skeletons lay in tens and twenties. At first, these successive heaps seemed strange, after twenty or thirty miles they grew terrible. (Murray 1967, 158).

The heyday of the road was in the Middle Ages but it was still a major trading route in the 1830s and 1840s. By the end of the nineteenth century, however, it had ceased to exist as a trade route, largely because of the abolition of slave trading. Without this gruesome and lucrative commodity the caravans were no longer profitable.

Figure 13. Ahmed Hassanein Bey.

The Egyptian explorer, A.M. Hassanein Bey (figure 13) captured the essence of the desert in his beautiful book *The Lost Oases (*1925). He appreciated its perils and its allure:

> It is as though a man were deeply in love with a very fascinating but cruel woman. She treats him badly, and the world crumples in his hand; at night she smiles on him and the whole world is a paradise. The desert smiles and there is no place on earth worth living in but the desert. (Hassanein Bey 1925, 25).

In stark contrast to the desert itself are the oases. These have always been pivots around which exploration can occur, and have been the only places where people can settle for any extended period. They form splashes of greenery, some with fields of alfalfa and date groves, many with swaying doum palms (also known as the gingerbread tree, *Hyphaene Thebaica*), and some with blue lakes and gushing springs. Ralph Bagnold had a particularly soft spot for Selima:

> There is something wonderfully friendly about a Libyan Desert oasis, with its deep greenery of palms and grass backed by the brown barren cliffs and roofed over by a cloudless blue sky….Selima is especially attractive – the oasis of a story-book, uninhabited by man and rarely visited, consisting of two little clumps of green palms, carpeted beneath with grass, and a small stone ruin of uncertain date. (Bagnold 1935, 177).

G.W. Murray (1967, 188) was struck by Siwa, which was "novel, fresh and blooming" as well as being "ancient, evil and African". However, the oasis dwellers were not always written about in the most flattering terms by British visitors. C.S. Jarvis (1936, 46) found the people of Kharga, of Berber strain, to be "degenerate and despondent", and attributed this to the prevalence of malaria. C.D. Belgrave was especially outspoken about the Siwans, the sexual proclivities of whom were deemed far too dire to be described in detail in the 1920s:

> The Siwans are typically Oriental. They are hospitable, dishonest, lazy, picturesque, ignorant, superstitious, cheerful, cunning, easily moved to joy or anger, fond of intrigue and ultra conservative. They are not immoral, they simply have no morals. The men are notoriously degenerate and resemble in their habits the Pathans of India. They seem to consider that every vice and indulgence is lawful. (Belgrave 1923, 149).

The Libyan Desert was an area of some political sensitivity, for the borders between the great colonial powers, which had come late to the area, were often ill-defined and sometimes contentious. In the east, the British held sway, with Egypt and the Suez Canal at a pivotal point between the

Figure 14. Britannia conquers the Nile.

Mediterranean and the Indian Empire (figure 14). The British acquired a majority shareholding in the canal in 1875, occupied Egypt (part of the Ottoman Empire) in 1882, declared it a protectorate in 1914, abolished the protectorate in 1922, then recognised it as an independent state, but kept control of the legal system, defence, communications and the Suez Canal.

To the south, since 1899, the Sudan was an Anglo-Egyptian Condominium, but the emphasis was on the Anglo. After Britain renounced its protectorate over Egypt, it assumed an even greater role in the Sudan, developing the civil service ('blacks and browns ruled by blues') and establishing the Sudan Defence Force to replace Egyptian units. In the west, the Italians, very late starters in the race for colonies, invaded Libya in 1911, but encountered severe resistance from local groups including the Sanussi of Cyrenaica (for more on the Sanussi see chapter on the Light Car Patrols below, p. 49). Until the end of the First World War, Italian forces, sometimes under conditions of siege, were confined to the coastal enclaves. However, with the accession to power of Mussolini's Fascist government in October 1922, the Italians embarked on a sometimes brutal mission to subdue the interior of Libya. This was completed only in 1931 when the last Sanussi stronghold, Kufra oasis, fell. The leader of the Sanussi resistance in Libya, Shaikh Umar al Mukthar, was captured, court-martialled and hanged before a crowd of 20,000 Arabs that had been assembled to witness the gruesome event. On 24 January 1932 General Badoglio announced that the rebellion in Cyrenaica had been defeated. According to official figures, a total of 6,484 rebels had been killed and 76,815 inhabitants interned, almost exactly half the total population of Cyrenaica (Gooch 2005). Even Italian statistics reveal a population decline from 225,000 in 1928 to 142,000 in 1931, largely because many Libyans went into exile in neighbouring countries. The Italian Kufra campaign, "a masterpiece of organisation", according to Bagnold, was partly achieved by the use of motor transport. Thereafter, the Italians, encouraged by the Italian Geographical Society, began to explore the interior, and the great explorer and geologist, Ardito Desio, drove as far as Murzuk, finding traces of oil in the process (Desio 1950).

In the south-west, in Chad, the French were the colonial power. They moved into the area in the 1890s onwards, but throughout the colonial period large areas of Chad were never governed effectively from Fort Lamy (now N'Djamena). Indeed, Chad did not receive separate colony status or a unified administrative policy until 1920, and even then was administered as part of French Equatorial Africa under the direction of a governor general stationed far away in Brazzaville in the French Congo. Chad was not a popular posting for French colonial officials, so posts often went to novices or to those out of favour. It was almost impossible to be too demented or depraved to be considered unfit for duty in Chad.

So, even in the 1920s and 1930s large tracts of the Libyan Desert were only recently under colonial control, were largely *terra incognita*, and had boundaries that were imperfectly delimited. This was especially true in the vicinity of Uweinat, a vital source of water inconveniently located at the borders of Egypt, Sudan and Libya. It is also important to remember just how far Uweinat was from the centres of colonial power: 1,750 km as the crow flies from Tripoli, 1,350 km from Cairo, 1,250 km from Fort Lamy and almost 1,000 km from Khartoum. Notwithstanding the barren nature of the terrain and the paucity of human population, the colonial powers were nervous about their distant boundaries and suspicious of the strategic ambitions of each other. The gathering of intelligence was a major priority and the motor car provided the means by which this might be acquired.

Cars had many advantages over the camel, as Michael Mason so clearly explained in the context of Bill Shaw's great expedition in the 1930s:

> The Ford car was the only thing to use. To one who naturally loathes and fears all machines except firearms, and loves and understands animals, this takes strength of mind to believe. But whereas the camel is certainly best over very rough going, over very soft sand, over short distances and when time is no object at all, the car has no rival in any long expedition in such a desert as that of Libya. For the spaces over which the snarling caravan will plod – day after day and week after week across the level sand – cars can cross in a matter of hours. Camels need water and fodder, Arabs to lead them, and occasional rest. The Arabs need food and water. All this means many camels to each white man. One car can carry two white men with everything that they need for weeks, and needs no rest. (Mason 1936, 18).

Claud Williams, one of those who chased the Sanussi, pointed out that a journey of just over 300 km with loaded camels, with no possibility of renewing food or water supplies en route, would occupy seven or eight days. He reckoned that the limit of endurance of the Bedouin camel is about eight days, so that the margin for error was very slight. As he remarked:

> If a man or beast falls sick, he must march or die. There can be no rest, loitering may mean a terrible death for the whole party. (Parker 2004, 46).

John Ball (1917) pointed out that a Model T car could travel five times further per day than a camel. However, some travellers regretted the advent of the motor car. Among these was W.J. Harding King, who had done a series of journeys in the vicinity of Kharga and Dakhla just before the First World War:

> The Libyan Desert, that in the past has to a great extent defied the efforts of all its explorers, is bound before long to give up its secrets. Suitably designed cars, accompanied perhaps by a scouting plane, our (*sic*) enemies against which even the most avid desert is almost defenceless, though one cannot but regret the necessity for such prosaic mechanical aids, they unquestionably afford an ideal method of conducting long pioneer explorations in a waterless desert. (Harding King 1925, 11).

Some travellers resolutely rejected the motor car or regretted their need to use it. Amongst these was Wilfred Thesiger, who drove jeeps in the desert in the Second World War when he was a member of the Special Air Service (SAS). He remarked (1987, 386) that in a jeep he could derive no pleasure from the desert itself; even the enormous sand dunes of the Erg left him unmoved; they were but another obstacle to be mechanically surmounted. However, even before the First World War other travellers explored the potential of the motor car and experimented with such devices as propellers (figure 15).

Prior to the motor car there had nonetheless been a number of important explorations of the Western Desert by camel. Particularly notable was Gerhard Rohlfs (1831-1896). A German, he initially trained as a doctor, but in 1855 he went to Algeria and enlisted in the Foreign Legion. He developed a fascination with Arabic, Islam and the Sahara, and travelled widely, often in disguise. He has sometimes been regarded as the German version of Sir Richard Burton. In 1873, the Khedive of Egypt invited this scholarly-looking man, with a carefully waxed moustache and nicely brushed goatee, to lead an expedition from Dakhla to Kufra. He could not reach his objective, and was forced to head towards Siwa though the Great Sand Sea. His grim account of this journey, of his privations, and of the

Figure 15. A propeller-driven car of 1912.

problems of the Sand Sea, were not such as to encourage future explorers. Nonetheless, subsequently, people like W.J. Harding King ranged widely in the northern parts of the Libyan desert, as did Wilfred ('Wiffy') Jennings-Bramly, who entered the walled city of Siwa in 1897. Jennings-Bramly undertook intelligence activities in Sinai before 1914, was involved in the Sanussi campaign of the First World War, created a Zoo in Giza (where he cleared visitors who overstayed their welcome by letting out a Russian Wolf), built a house to the west of Alexandria, and during the Second World War resisted all Army advice to leave. He was one of those people who through their long residence in the desert provided advice to generations of subsequent travellers.

The Light Car Patrols

The origins of motoring in the Western Desert go back to the First World War with the formation of the Light Car Patrols. These were established by the British in Egypt, under the command of General Sir Archibald Murray (Gordon 1987, 2) to combat incursions by the Sanussi. The Sanussi were in the words of Hassanein Bey (1925, 56) "not a race nor a country, nor a political entity, nor a religion" but had some of the characteristics of all four. They were founded by Muhammed ibn Ali al-Sanusi (1785 or 1787-1859) and were a Sufi brotherhood based in Libya and the Central Sahara. Their core area was among the Bedouin of Cyrenaica, in what is now eastern Libya. In 1895, they established their centre at the secret oasis of Kufra. When the Italians invaded Libya in 1911, the Sanussi leader, Ahmad al-Sharif – the Grand Sanussi – raised the call for a *Jihad* and led a force against the invaders. The Grand Sanussi was regarded by the British as a vainglorious lover of luxury who always fled on the first shot being fired or on a report that the British were coming (Massey 1918). In 1915, because the British were allies of the Italians and as a result of encouragement from the Turks and the Germans, the Sanussi went on to attack the British in Egypt. In due course they had to be dislodged from the coastal strip between Sollum and Mersa Matruh, and the interior oases of Dakhla, Bahariya and Siwa (Massey 1918).

The Sanussi advanced as far as Mersa Matruh, a town on the Mediterranean coast some 300 km west of Alexandria, and for more than a year they threatened Egypt with invasion (McGuirk 2007). Thousands of British and Empire troops, badly needed in Palestine and elsewhere, were tied up. Forts were built, and their gaunt, ruined outlines can still be seen on the skyline at strategically important locations, such as the cliffs behind the oasis of Bahariya. In the environment of the Western Desert traditional horse-borne yeomanry were unable to operate effectively,

Figure 16. A Model T Ford of the Light Car Patrols.

as they were too far from fodder and water. It was for this reason that the Light Car Patrols (LCPs) were established.

There were fifteen patrols in all, formed from elements of the Machine Gun Corps, the Army Service Corps and Australian and New Zealand personnel. With the help of a government geologist, Dr John Ball (1874-1941), they invented the sun compass to enable them to navigate featureless desert and made the first condensers – they called them 'water economizers' – to reduce water loss from their boiling radiators. The cars they used were 20 hp, four-cylinder Model T Fords (figure 16), fitted with what were then regarded as 'oversized' three-and-a-half-inch (9 cm) tyres. These were, by modern standards, horribly narrow for motoring in sand. Nonetheless, with these simple but robust machines, which had the benefit of a high ground clearance and a relatively high power to weight ratio (15 cwt), the LCPs showed for the first time what cars could achieve in desert travel.

With crews of three and rations for three days, the Fords could go practically anywhere a camel could. They were sufficiently well armed to form a valuable adjunct to larger armed vehicles, while their mobility gave them a great advantage over enemy foot-soldiers and camel-borne troops.

It was one of the LCPs, commanded by Captain Claud H. Williams MC, of the Pembroke Yeomanry, that undertook an aneroid survey which gave an inkling for the first time of the existence of the great Qattara Depression (Anon. 1965). Williams was a great devotee of the Model T, and noted that its ability to allow gear changes to be made easily and rapidly was a tremendous virtue in sandy country, where any loss of pace as one changed down, could be a cause of getting stuck. Other cars at the time often had less amenable gearboxes. He also remarked that "It is difficult to put a Ford car out of action" (Williams 1919, 123), though he did note that after a moist night or a sand-storm they could be tricky to start in the morning. Tyre life was also limited and averaged only 2,400 to 4,800 km under normal desert conditions – perhaps a tenth of what one might expect today. Oil consumption was also considerable, particularly if the engine got hot and waste through the gaskets increased. He reckoned that 1.7 litres of oil were required every 160 km. Nevertheless, he argued (Ibid., 131), "With complete equipment and proper preparation there is hardly any limit to what Ford cars can accomplish in the desert". He remarked that "The Ford has as many lives as a cat", and was impressed by the fact that they still ran even when the engine was held on by wire, leaky radiators plugged with chewing gum, wheels spliced with bits of petrol case, and holes plugged with corks. "You can't", he remarked, "kill a Ford Car" (Williams undated, 84-5).

As Ralph Bagnold was later to write in his *Libyan Sands:*

...in 1916 a tiny force of Light Car Patrols, armed with machine guns, guarded the whole 800-mile frontier against a possible recrudescence of the Sanussi menace. These patrols covered great distances of unknown waterless and lifeless country...and among other things they succeeded in mapping, with the aid of speedometer readings and compass bearings a great part of the northern desert....Their exploits, with the crude vehicles they had, were astonishing. The old tracks made by their unsuitable narrow tyres can be seen to this day, very faintly, far out even beyond the Oases several hundred miles from the Nile. (Bagnold 1935, 13).

Bagnold remarked that sometimes one could even see the sites of their misadventures: deeper ruts surrounded by vague old footmarks in the soft gravelly sand, where the cars stuck and had to be pushed out by hand.

Claud Williams gives a graphic account of their first operation from Wadi Natrun to Bahariya, during which they captured a group of Bedouin travelling with an assortment of automatic pistols, dynamite and some detonators. These "naughty men", intent on carrying out assassinations of Egyptian officials, were duly punished. Two of them were shot. He was rather modest about the great triumph of removing the Sanussi from Siwa, describing the actual battle as an "opera bouffe" (Williams undated, 16), and "a very safe and entertaining performance to have been mixed up in." He called it "the Siwa stunt".

The Light Car Patrols (figure 17) were largely disbanded after the end of the Sanussi campaign, though some of the vehicles were transferred to the newly formed Frontier District Administration. The history of their exploits was never fully written up, though Claud Williams did produce a book in 1919, for long classified by the military authorities because of its great potential strategic importance, called *Report on the Military Geography of the North-Western Desert of Egypt.* This small, khaki book gives details of routes, native caravan tracks (*masrabs*) and passes, particularly in the Siwa area, suggestions about the best oil and petrol containers, advice about the need to carry a canvas cover to put over the car and its passengers during the heat of the day, the recommendation that acetylene lights were better than electric as they did not suddenly dim when engine revs fell, the maximum safe load per car (*c.* 550 kg), and ways of constructing condensers and sun compasses. He also produced an undated typescript,

Figure 17. A Model T Ford Light Car Patrol in the First World War.

now held in the RGS archives, that describes some of the routes covered, to Bahariya, Siwa, Benghazi and beyond. Many of these routes followed old *masrabs.* Williams described them:

> They consist of wavy camel tracks a few feet apart, running parallel to one another, and varying in number from five or six to fifty or sixty, according to the importance of the route....The course of a large masrab is generally marked at frequent intervals with camel bones and with human graves, which testify to the toll which the desert exacts from intruders into its solitudes. These, especially the tiny graves, present a rather pathetic appearance to the traveller by motor-car who traverses in an hour what would be a wearisome day's journey on camel back or on foot. (de Cosson 1935, 159).

The journey he made to Benghazi and the Sanussi centre of Zuetina was a round trip of just under 2,000 km.

The Light Car Patrols never achieved much fame, though for a while some landmarks carried their names on maps – Owston's Dunes, Williams's Dunes, Partridge Gap or Wilson Peak. Williams (undated, 1) attributed this lack of fame to the fact that they were operating in a quiet battle front, were small in number, had casualty lists that were almost nil, and undertook work that was unspectacular. They were, however, undoubtedly innovative:

> At first we were a bit shy about venturing very far afield. It seemed easy to get lost or to smash cars, or to run short of petrol or water; but we soon gained confidence in our ability to provide for all our needs. As a mere precaution we began to plot our course as we went. We learnt to use compass and speedometer with skill and accuracy, and evolved a simple device for using the sun's shadow as a means of keeping a good direction. Soon we found ourselves able to make a far more accurate dead reckoning than on a ship at sea; we began to chart our information and to build up gradually a fairly reliable map of the country. (Ibid., 5).

In this endeavour he was doubtless assisted by the surveyor, John Ball, whom he described affectionately as 'The Little Doctor'. Ball for his part, though generally dismissive of the capabilities of soldiers as topographers, made an exception for Williams (Jarvis 1938, 88).

Claud Williams saw the Light Car Patrols as a substitute for cavalry:

> We could bunch several patrols together and handle them as one unit under one leader. A few waves of the signalling flag would split the force into sections, advance them, retire them, wheel them, shift them from position to position, and bring them, in short, into almost as great a variety of formations as can be done with a squadron of cavalry. On that fine open country, such a force, able to strike, and to strike hard and often at a distance of hundreds of miles and for weeks at a time, formed the best possible protection against further trouble with the western Arabs. (Williams undated, 79).

The troops with the patrols had to be versatile (Ibid., 77). They had to be "soldier, chauffeur, mechanic, blood-hound, surveyor, signaller, astronomer and a few hundred other trades and callings."

The end of cavalry as a mode of warfare was in sight. The last use of cavalry as a strategic mass was to take place in the Middle East in 1917, when Allenby, the Commander-in-Chief of the Egyptian Expeditionary Force in Egypt and Palestine, used it to defeat the Turks on his way to occupy Damascus.

Claud Williams himself is an obscure figure, though the inhabitants of Bahariya still draw attention to the dark, stone-built 'English House' which he constructed on a promontory on the Black Hill above the oasis. He was a pipe-smoking, New Zealand sheep farmer who enlisted in the British Army in 1915 and was stationed in the Egyptian Desert by April 1916. He died in New Zealand in his nineties (Harold 2003), giving a foretaste of the longevity of many of the desert's explorers. Ardito Desio, the greatest of the Italian explorers of the desert, lived to be 104.

Claud Williams (figure 18) appears to have had an ambivalent attitude to the desert. On the one hand he called it "hateful, cruel, pitiless", and remarked that "there is literally nothing to recommend this country". He found the few scattered inhabitants of the more favoured parts to be "squalid, miserable-looking specimens". The scenery could be "distinctly gruesome in its desolation". He remarked that "A remarkable feature of the desert is the absence of remarkable features…you may travel many a weary hundred miles for ever and ever amen". On the other hand, he refers to the intense fascination that the desert exercises, the beauty of sun rise and sun set, the pure and vivid colouring of oasis lakes, and the attractive antics of that rampant rodent, the jerboa or desert rat (Parker 2004, 42-46).

The Model T Ford, with which the Light Car Patrols were equipped, was built by the Ford Company. Formed in 1903, Ford began production of the Model T in September 1908 at the Piquette Plant in Detroit. It was designed to be lightweight, flexible and simple. Initially it was assembled by hand, but subsequently Ford introduced an assembly line system said to have been the brainchild of William C. Klann, who had obtained the idea on a visit to the slaughterhouse at Chicago's Union Stock yards,

Figure 18a. Claud Williams at the wheel of a stripped-down Model T Ford of the Light Car Patrols.

Figure 18b. The Light Car Patrols.

where animals were butchered as they moved along a conveyor. As a result Ford cars came off the assembly line in three minute intervals, required less labour to manufacture, and became increasingly cheap. It initially cost $850, but by the 1920s the price had fallen to just $300. By 1915 sales exceeded half a million and over a production period of 19 years, more than 15 million 'Tin Lizzies' were produced, most in Dearborn near Detroit, but others elsewhere, such as at Trafford Park in Manchester, England. By the time Ford made his ten millionth car, nine out of ten cars in the entire world were Fords.

The Model T had a 2,896-cc, 20-hp, 4-cylinder engine, with just 2 forward gears and a reverse. It had a design top speed of 45 mph (72 kph). It was a rear-wheel drive design with very different controls than those found in a modern car. Its transmission was controlled with three foot pedals and a lever mounted to the left of the driver's seat. The throttle was controlled with a lever on the steering wheel. There was no separate clutch pedal and braking was achieved through the transmission rather than by using calliper brakes on the wheels: the right foot pedal applied a band around a drum in the transmission, thus stopping the rear wheels from turning. Furthermore, because fuel relied on gravity to flow forward from the fuel tank to the carburettor, a Model T could not climb a steep hill when the fuel level was low. One solution was to go up steep hills in reverse. The suspension was rudimentary, and consisted of a transversely mounted semi-elliptical spring for each of the front and rear axles. Wheels were originally wooden artillery wheels. On the other hand, Ford used high quality vanadium steel for some of the components and the car had a remarkable reputation for durability.

At the beginning of the First World War, Henry Ford initially refused to let his cars be used in combat conditions, but eventually changed his mind. The British purchased about 19,000 of these cars during the war, and armed with a Lewis gun (an automatic machine gun), they were used not only in North Africa (figure 19), but also in Palestine, Mesopotamia, and France. The Model T remained in production until 1927, when Henry Ford

Figure 19. Bottoms up! A Ford bogged down. Notice the narrow tyres and box body.

closed his plants for 7 months to switch production to another stalwart of desert travel, The Model A, which first appeared in December 1927. A change of model came none too soon: 1927 was the year that Chevrolet outsold Ford for the first time.

As to the Sanussi, their efforts were a failure and their leader, the Grand Sheik Sayyid Ahmed, was compelled to take flight to Constantinople in a German submarine. However, his successor, Sayed Mohammed Idris, proved to be a staunch encourager of desert exploration and he helped Ahmed Mohammed Hassenein Bey to make his journey to the forbidden oasis of Kufra in 1920/21 with Rosita Forbes.

However, the days of the Light Car Patrols were not without their salutary reminder of the perils of desert motoring that such expeditions would face. As C.J. Jarvis related:

In 1921 an Army Light Car Patrol set out with four cars from Sollum to go to Siwa....About fifteen miles out from Sollum one of the cars, driven by a sergeant, developed some slight trouble and the patrol went on, telling him to follow. It was then late in the afternoon, and the intention was to run for a matter of another hour only before camping for the night. What actually happened after this has never been satisfactorily cleared up – apparently the sergeant, after he had restarted his car, ran southwards for some hours and, failing to find petrol, returned on his tracks to Sollum. (Jarvis 1936, 122).

The hapless sergeant was then in a terrible state.

He appears to have lost his head through terror of the desert and to have driven the car into a stone cairn by the side of the road, smashing the radiator and letting the water out. The sergeant and the two privates then started to walk in to Sollum and, according to the account of the men, the sergeant became demented and shot himself. As he was only wounded, they admitted that they had fired into his head to finish him off, and ultimately they were found – at the last gasp – crawling into Sollum...

What proved to be particularly ghastly about this tragedy was that when their water-bottles were emptied it was found that in their terror of thirst, they had filled them with the blood of the dead man.

The Duke of Westminster
and the Rolls Royce armoured cars

Other larger vehicles were also used by Commonwealth forces during the war. Notable were the steel war chariots – armoured cars – commanded and partly designed by the second Duke of Westminster (then a major), Sir Hugh Richard Arthur Grosvenor (figure 20). He was immensely rich – one of the richest men in what was then the richest country on Earth. He had wintered in Egypt in 1912, playing polo and socialising, but on the outbreak of the First World War he became a staff officer in the army, developed an interest in armour plating automobiles for military use, served in France until the end of 1915, and was then sent to Egypt.

The armoured cars he used and developed were described by an aptly named man who was later to be Lawrence of Arabia's driver – S.C. Rolls. These consisted of a 40-50 hp Rolls Royce Alpine Chassis, fitted with four-speed gearing, and with a specially strengthened back axle. Originally they had been sent to Egypt for use by the Royal Navy Air Service (Gordon 1987, 5). Indeed, their revolving gun turret was an essentially naval feature. Rolls described these remarkable vehicles in detail:

> ...there was mounted a steel cylinder, five feet in diameter, fitted with a revolving turret, and this formed the principal part of the body. Behind it there was an open platform made of wood. The cylinder, the bonnet, the doors covering the front of the radiator, and other details were of specially toughened bullet-proof armour plate, three-eights of an inch thick. In the turret, which formed the roof of the cylinder, a Vickers-Maxim gun was mounted, its breach end extending a foot into the interior. The heat in the Libyan desert in summer was found to be so great that men inside the cars were in danger of being cooked like rabbits in a saucepan... (Rolls 1937, 22).

Figure 20. Hugh Richard Arthur Grosvenor, 2nd Duke of Westminster (1879-1953).

The conditions for the crews were extremely restricted and this presented a problem, not least for their noble commander, who had a striking resemblance to British Prime Minister Harold Macmillan:

Only short men could stand upright in the cylinder; and tall men, who had to half double themselves up, took up very much more room and

WHEELS ACROSS THE DESERT

were always cramped and uncomfortable, and on this account were generally considered the least desirable to work with. Even small men had to crouch when firing the Maxim or a rifle. Most of our fellows were short, and the great height of the Duke of Westminster no doubt added a trial to his pains and fatigues such as the rest of us were spared. (Ibid.).

Another problem was tyres:

We had great difficulty in obtaining suitable wheels for the cars. At first we tried filling the tires with rubber solution, but this was soon given up, as the moment a tire was damaged by bullets or sharp stones the rubber solution escaped. We also used both single and double wheels at different times. (Ibid.).

The Rolls cars (figure 21) were not easy to drive. Indeed, Major T.I. Dun of the 12th Royal Lancers, who travelled with them from Cairo to Siwa, called them "fleeting pillboxes" (Dun 1933, 20). With their great weight of armour plating and the momentum provided by a heavy gun and turret, they had a habit of careering over onto their sides if one of the front wheels hit a large obstacle. The crew outside would tend to be thrown clear, but those inside could receive head wounds from the projecting metal parts. For the most part the Duke preferred to drive and lead his squadron in his own open Rolls Royce, which though armed with a machine gun, offered very little protection.

The exploits of the Duke of Westminster's armoured cars were remarkable. In spite of their prodigious use of fuel and water, their tendency to bog down in soft sand, and their need for an elaborate train of support vehicles, their dash to Siwa in early 1917, and its subsequent capture, put an end to Sanussi resistance. Their actions had many of the qualities of a brilliant old-style cavalry charge. The difference was that no horsed cavalry could have made so rapid a move across desert or stormed enemy machine guns and artillery without taking punishing casualties.

Figure 21. A Mark 1 Rolls Royce armoured car of 1920 in the Bovington Tank Museum, Dorset.

Figure 22. The Duke in his own open armoured Rolls Royce.

Most remarkable of all, however, was the rescue of British hostages from two ships, HMS *Moorina* and HMS *Tara*, whose crews, having been sunk by German submarines, were brought ashore and handed over to the local Arabs by the Germans. The prisoners were in a very bad way, exhausted and emaciated, and forced to supplement their meagre diet of rice (all Cyrenaic starved that winter) with snails and carrion:

> A force of armoured cars and other cars, under the command of the Duke of Westminster, set off…from Sollum with a native guide. They dashed across the desert to Bir Hakim, rescued the prisoners and brought them back to Sollum, having travelled across some 120 miles of unknown desert and attacked an enemy whose numbers they did not know. This gallant enterprise was perhaps the most brilliant affair which occurred during the operations on the Western Desert. (Belgrave 1923, 130-131).

The Duke of Westminster (figure 22) received the DSO for his exploit, and was recommended for the Victoria Cross. The recommendation was not sanctioned in London, either because it was blocked by Field Marshal Lord Kitchener (then Secretary of State for War, whom the Duke did not like), or because in the view of Winston Churchill, then Minister of Munitions, the proposal came simply because he was a Duke. Nicknamed 'Bend'Or', he married four times, had various lovers, including 'Coco' Chanel, espoused right wing views, and loathed homosexuals about as much as he loved the Empire (Ridley 1985). He 'outed' his own brother-in-law, William, the 7th Earl Beauchamp.

Hassanein Bey and Rosita Forbes

Ahmed Hassanein (later Pasha) was a member of the Turkish ruling class in Egypt, who was captain of the Egyptian team at the Brussels Olympic Games in 1920, and, enjoying the patronage of King Fouad I and his son, Farouk, became an influential figure in palace affairs. Born in Cairo in 1889, where his father was a distinguished scholar at the thousand year old mosque of al-Azhar, he was educated at Balliol, an Oxford college that was at the time regarded by itself and by outsiders as an intellectual power house. There he was a friend of Francis Rodd and together they served during the First World War on the British mission to the Sanussis. It was then that they conceived the idea of going to Kufra, but in the event Rodd dropped out and was replaced by Rosita Forbes (figure 23). During the trip this divorced woman, strikingly handsome, with dark hair and eyes, and known in London for her huge Ascot hats, high heels and sophisticated make-up, dressed as a Muslim female and posed as a relative of Hassanein. She took the name of Khadija and invented a Circassian mother to account for her imperfect Arabic. It is said that she tried, unsuccessfully, to seduce him but it is also said he resisted her advances.

Mrs Forbes, who withstood the hardships of this and other journeys with great stamina and laudable fortitude, is often accused of writing up the expedition, magnifying her own role and downplaying that of her Egyptian colleague. This was a cause of sorrow to her Egyptian host, who was not a mere dragoman as he believed she had portrayed him. It was alleged in *The Times* that Hassanein Bey had told the Royal Scottish Geographical Society that it was he who had originated the idea of the expedition, that he had organised it, and that it was 'his' expedition, but various people, including the hugely influential D.G. Hogarth, came to Rosita's defence. Hogarth credited her with "most of the preparation" and believed she was the "driving force throughout" (*The Times*, 9 December, 1921). Rosita's own account of the expedition in *The Times,* however, says very little about her companion.

Figure 23. Rosita Forbes.

In the first half of 1923, Hassanein Bey made his great camel trek, the climax of pre-car desert crossings, from Sollum on the Mediterranean to El Obeid in Sudan. He trekked 3,500 km over seven months and 23 days (map 5). For this he was awarded a gold medal by the Royal Geographical Society (RGS) in London (Ball, 1924, 366). The trip established the true location of some major landmarks of the Western Desert, including Kufra, Arkenu and Uweinat. As John Ball, head of the Egyptian Government's Desert Survey Department, stated:

I may be permitted to remark that his expedition appears to me to be an almost unique achievement in the annals of geographical exploration. The journey of 3,345 kms, from Sollum to El Obeid, most of it through inhospitable deserts sparsely inhabited by fanatical and predatory tribes, is one which, without a

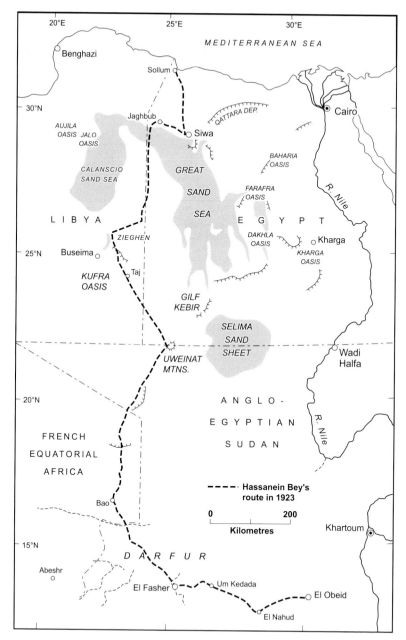

Map 5. Hassanein Bey's great journey of 1923.

strong military escort, could have been undertaken only by a Moslem, and by one of remarkable grit, tact, and perseverance. But Hassenein Bey has not only accomplished this difficult journey and brought back interesting descriptions and photographs of the country through which he passed. (Ball 1924, 385).

Ball, a stickler for correct procedures, was particularly impressed by the surveying skills that had been learnt, for before setting out from Cairo Hassanein Bey had applied himself strenuously for several weeks to acquiring facility in the use of the theodolite, and instruction in the particular methods of reconnaissance-survey best adapted for exploration of the kind on which he was to embark. Throughout his travels he made excellent use of the surveying knowledge thus acquired and managed somehow to carry out all this observations single-handed, and to maintain the continuity and accuracy of his measurements and records over the distance of the more than 2,000 km which separates the points on his route whose positions were previously known.

Hassanein Bey found many rock pictures at Uweinat and these excited many later explorers to visit the area. In America, gripped by the Rudolf Valentino film, *The Sheik,* he became a celebrity. In Egypt his explorations were regarded as a patriotic achievement. He was feted at a ceremony in the Cairo Opera House, where King Fuad conferred on him the title of *bey.* In 1927 the British made him a Knight Commander of the Victorian Order. They also inadvertently killed him, for in February 1946 he died in a freak motor accident when a British truck went into a skid and smashed into his car on a rain-swept Cairo bridge (Haag 2006).

The rock drawings that Hassanein Bey found at Uweinat were in some cases actual paintings and in other cases were engravings that had been scratched or engraved into the rock surface. In desert regions a patina often develops on boulders and rock outcrops – 'desert varnish' – and it tends to be dark in colour, being composed of the oxides of iron and manganese. Thus when it is removed, the lighter coloured underlying rock is exposed and so a striking image can be created. Subsequently, Kemal El Din also found new examples, which reminded the Abbé Breuil (the French Archaeologist and Anthropologist) of the bushmen (San) paintings of southern Africa. Others (including the famous 'Cave of Swimmers') were discovered by László Almásy, Leo Frobenius, Lodovio di Caporiacco, Ralph Bagnold, Ronald Peel, Bill Shaw and H.A. Winkler (Peel 1939).

Prince Kemal el Din
and the Citroën half-tracks

As Hassanein Bey's exploits demonstrate, there were some Egyptians who made notable contributions to the exploration of the desert. It was far from being the preserve of British chaps. Among these there was Prince Hussein Kemal el Din (sometimes Kemal el-Dine), son of the Khedive Ismail (figure 24). In 1917, he declined an offer from the British to succeed his late father to the Egyptian throne, largely because he had little interest in politics, but a great deal of interest in travel and big game shooting. He made many camel journeys but in 1923 he joined up with two British stalwarts, Dr John Ball (Director of the Desert Surveys Department) and Major C.S. Jarvis (who had been in the Light Car Patrols with Captain Williams). Setting aside any patriotic misgivings, they used a fleet of French Citroën caterpillar or halftrack vehicles (*autochenilles*) (figure 25) and box Fords. The Prince's personal wealth, which was very considerable, provided the necessary finance.

The Prince made a series of automobile expeditions between 1923 and 1926 (Kemal el Din 1928, 174). The first, in March 1923, left from Kharga Oasis. This was a regular starting and finishing point for many journeys described in this book. Today, as a consequence of the so-called New Valley scheme, Kharga has large expanses of drab, cracked, baking, concrete apartment blocks reminiscent of the Soviet era in Eastern Europe. However, in the early decades of the twentieth century, set in magnificent shady date groves, it was "a picturesque compact conglomeration of houses, built of sun-dried bricks, and of every shape and size." Llewellyn Beadnell in *An Egyptian Oasis* (1909, 67) remarked that its streets meandered in a very remarkable manner, required a guide to navigate their intricate network, and were to a large extent in partial or total darkness, owing to their being for the most part covered by upper storeys. The reason why Kharga was often selected, apart from the fact that it offered an assured

Figure 24. Kemal al Din.

Figure 25. Caterpillar tractors carrying heavy loads over a sand dune between Bir Terfawi and Uweinat, photographed by Dr John Ball.

supply of water at the northern end of the Darb Al Arba'in, was that it was served by a railway that ran westwards from the Nile Valley. The narrow gauge line, only 75 cm wide, was built in 1909 by the Corporation of Western Egypt Limited in the hope that it would help them to develop their concessions in the oasis. Small steam locomotives, built in Leeds, hauled trains in and out of the oasis once or twice a week. The Corporation failed to find the water and minerals it had hoped for, and its plan to set up ostrich farms at Dakhla was never a success. Without the Corporation the railway was also not commercially viable, but it was taken over by the Government of Egypt and its existence did mean that cars and supplies could be carried from the Nile Valley into the desert, saving a great deal of driving and removing the need to motor down the precipitous limestone slopes and wind-blasted plateau to the east of the oasis. The route, now abandoned, is easily traced. It is a haunting monument to misguided Edwardian optimism and the skill and perseverance of the railway engineer.

From Kharga, the expedition headed still further westwards towards the edge of the Great Sand Sea. Its intention was to find a cairn and message left by the German explorer, Rohlfs, on 8 February 1874, which indicated the most westerly point he had reached on his epic journey from Dakhla to Kufra. This point was called 'Regenfeld' on account of the rain shower Rohlfs experienced there. The expedition returned to Kharga without having found the cairn or the document. The second, in December 1923 (map 6) went from Cairo to the oasis of Baharia and back. The third, in January 1924, was a more ambitious affair, and departed from Cairo towards Dakhla Oasis and then on to Regenfeld, where, second time lucky, Rohlfs's document was located. The fourth, in the winter of 1924/5 ran from Kharga via Cheb and Tarfawi to Uweinat, and then down to the frontier of French Equatorial Africa and on to Merga in the Sudan. The singular Ball was once again involved.

In the following season 1925/6, another trip also left Kharga, and went as far west as Sarra. It was on this journey that the Prince named and encountered the imposing sandstone plateau of the Gilf Kebir

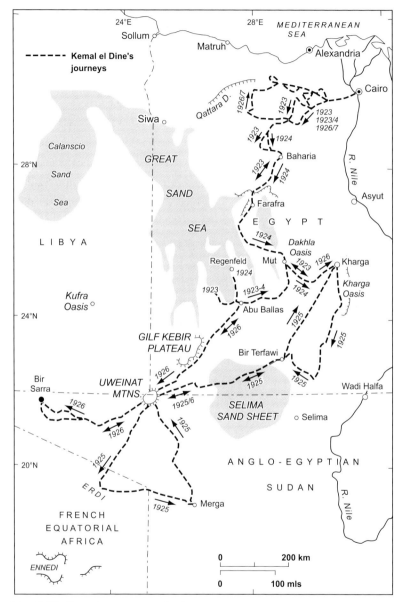

Map 6. The Prince's journeys in the desert.

(the Great Wall). One of his team, M. de Mascarel, also produced a relatively detailed topographic map of Uweinat.

The Prince, in his remarkable series of journeys, had not made any major ingress into the great dunes of the Great Sand Sea and was of the opinion "that it was quite out of the question for cars to penetrate the Sand Sea, let alone to cross the actual dunes." (Bagnold 1935, 166).

The Citroëns with their rubber caterpillar tracks were not without their problems. As C.S Jarvis remarked:

> They were the last word in desert transport in those days, as they would climb any sand-dune and, despite the small size of their engines, could develop enough power to drag another car out of the sand. But they had two great disadvantages – they could never travel faster than fifteen miles an hour even in good going, and their cooling apparatus was not up to the heat developed by the engine, so that they consumed vast quantities of water. (Jarvis 1936, 106).

By contrast, the Fords, which were the ordinary two-gear models of those days, had already proved their worth in sand. Owing to their very high horse-power compared with their weight, they could travel through heavy going better than any car on the market at that time. The Fords could always average about 56 kph on good going.

From then on, until Chevrolets and Willys Jeeps appeared in the Second World War, Fords were the preferred choice for most desert travellers.

The use of the Citroën cars almost exactly paralleled their use by the French to create a route from Algeria to Timbuktu. In 1922 M. André Citroën planned and organized what the French called a 'raid' across the Sahara, the object being to test his newly derived 'caterpillar' cars and to link the Upper (French) reaches of the Niger River and Mediterranean territories. The Citroën works produced a small fleet of 10 hp tractor cars, armed with machine guns in case of attack from the untamed inhabitants of the desert. The expedition set off from Touggourt (Algeria) on 17 December 1922. All five cars entered Timbuktu just 20 days later on 7 January 1923, having traversed 3,500 km of immensity. With much Gallic pomp and ceremony, the first trans-Saharan mail delivered by car, was handed over to Colonel Mangeot, the local regional commander. An immense crowd that had gathered under conditions of stifling heat greeted the occasion with thunderous applause. It was:

> …a motley crowd of all the races of the Soudan, from the veiled Tuareg, the Berabishes and the Moors with pointed profiles and long fuzzy hair to the negroes with enormous muscles, whose naked flesh exhaled the curious odour of stags. (Haardt and Audouin-Dubreuil 1924, 129).

A fast camel caravan would have needed at least six months to accomplish the same crossing (Wellard 1964, 308). The rubber caterpillar tracks were designed by Adolphe Kégresse and the team was led by Georges-Marie Haardt, general manager of the Citroën factories, and Louis Audouin-Dubreuil, who had commanded a group of machine gun cars attached to the Saharian squadrons in southern Tunisia. Among those who also completed the crossing was the expedition mascot, Flossie, a Sealyham terrier. Between 28 October 1924 and 26 June 1925, and encouraged by the success of this first raid, Citroëns accomplished a crossing of Africa from Algeria all the way to the Cape of Good Hope. The exploration of the Sahara by French and other teams using Renault and Citroën half-tracks has been described in great detail and with considerable deftness by Werner Nöther (2003)

The Prince died prematurely. During one of his final desert expeditions he contracted an infection which meant that his right leg had to be amputated and in February 1932, while on holiday in the South of France, he died, aged 58. Although buried in the Mokatam Hills, overlooking the Nile in Cairo, a cairn and a monument in his honour are fittingly erected at the most southernmost end of the Gilf Kebir. His travelling companion C.S. Jarvis described him thus:

He was a man of infinite charm and possessed all the characteristics of the Egyptian Royal family – a very quick and brilliant intelligence, a wonderful memory and the most extraordinary general knowledge of men and things. There was no topic discussed on the expedition that failed to bring forth an anecdote from the Prince's store, and he was equally at home whether one talked of the rival merits of shorthorn and South Devon cattle in England or the methods of dry-farming in Australia. His tragic death from blood-poisoning in 1932 was a very real loss to his country, for despite the fact that he did not mix in politics, he was a great personality and power in the land. (Jarvis 1936, 114).

Jarvis also records that travelling with the Prince had certain compensations. After a difficult day on the margins of the Great Sand Sea the Prince produced the necessary store to improve morale:

Dinner that night was memorable for two reasons. Firstly the cook came up with that charming smile which always accompanies bad news to announce that the whisky was finished. There is a perpetual dead silence in the sand dune country of Libya, but the awful hush that fell upon the surrounding country after this remark was penetrating enough to spread as far north as Cairo, stilling for one moment the honk-honk of dago-driven cars. The Prince, however, stepped into the breach – there was no situation with which he could not deal. "'I'm sorry about the whisky," he said, "but I brought with me a dozen brandy in case of illness."

A bottle was produced and the label looked familiar – that is to say I have seen it before on those rare occasions when I have dined at the tables of the great. Could it really be Napoléon? It was... (Ibid., 118-9).

This magnificent brandy had to be consumed from tin mugs, but still tasted wonderful. Then Jarvis moves on to describe the food that was produced:

The other event of note was a game pie made by the Prince's chef in Cairo, which contained nothing but the breasts of snipe made into a paste with truffles. This was certainly the most wonderful thing I have eaten in my life...(Ibid.).

Major Jarvis

Major Claude Scudamore Jarvis, CMG OBE (1879-1953), who travelled with Ball and the Prince Kemal el Din, was a military man who served in France, Palestine and Egypt in the First World War (figure 26). While Sub-District Commandant of Mariut, which lies in the Libyan Desert some 30 km west of Alexandria, he saw service at Mersa Matruh and accompanied a section of the Light Car Patrols in their box Fords, vulgarly called 'Flying Bedsteads'. In 1920 he was offered the post of District Commissioner in the oases of Kharga, Dakhla, Baharia and Farafra, with his headquarters in Kharga. He accepted with some trepidation because of the town's totally justified reputation for heat and mosquitoes and because he was scared of its impact on his wife, newly out from England. In 1923 he joined Dr Ball and Prince Kemal el Din on their great expedition but at the end of it decided that enough was enough:

Personally I have no wish to see this desert again – it is a harsh and forbidding area and now it has been proved to hide nothing of interest and is denied absolutely of life, I fail to see its attraction. (Jarvis 1936, 120).

In particular, Jarvis disliked the sand storms he encountered:

The car was a patrol Model T Ford without a windscreen, and so I put on a balaclava helmet and goggles to protect my face and eyes, and donned my gauntlets to cover my hands. I drove against the full force of that gale for four hours, finding it extremely difficult to see anything during the last hour. The reason for this was that my goggles, when I arrived eventually, were of that type of frosted glass one finds in lavatory windows, my leather gauntlets looked like soft chamois with the dark brown surface completely removed, whilst the radiator, bonnet and even the dull black front axle of the car were as highly burnished as if they were of chromium plated steel. (Jarvis 1943, 148).

Figure 26. Major C.S. Jarvis.

Luckily, for our story, not all British military men took such a view, but those who did were subsequently dubbed "The Short Range Desert Group". Jarvis set off for Sinai where he was the British *mudir* (governor) for 13 years, retiring in 1936. He was a wonderfully witty writer, writing under his own name or his pseudonym, Rameses, though sometimes his humour is at the expense of the indigenous inhabitants of the areas in which he served. That said, he became a legendary figure for this knowledge of Arabic and Bedouin customs and laws. Moreover, his satirical barbs were also directed at British officialdom. Most importantly, as was Dr Ball, he was recognised by Bagnold as one of his inspirations. Jarvis and Ball were both men of small physical stature but of great mental powers.

THE LITTLE DOCTOR: JOHN BALL

Dr John Ball (1872-1941), was one of the first enthusiasts for motor transport and was one of the most accomplished British scientific explorers of all time (figure 27). He has never received the appreciation he deserves, though he features as 'John Bell' in Michael Ondaatje's *The English Patient*.

He had one of the longest careers in the Western Desert, having joined the Egyptian Survey Department in 1897. A highly qualified geologist, engineer, surveyor and explorer, he had trained at the Royal College of Science and the Royal School of Mines in London, as well as in Freiberg and the University of Zurich. He was described by Ralph Bagnold, to whom he gave great assistance, as "the father of all modern investigations of the Libyan Desert" (Bagnold 1935, 95). Barely five feet (1.5 m) tall and almost totally deaf, he had at the turn of the century carried out surveys in the depressions of the Western Desert and elsewhere. These led to books on Kharga, Bahariya and Kurkur. In the First World War, as we have seen, he travelled with the Light Car Patrols, prepared numerous maps for the Egyptian Expeditionary Force, helped to develop sun compasses and condensers and subsequently accompanied Prince Kemal el Din on his great expeditions. In 1917, with the Light Car Patrols, he discovered 'Pottery Hill' (Abu Ballas), skirted the southern edge of the Great Sand Sea, and reached the broken foothills of the Gilf Kebir without, however, recognising the true nature of the great sandstone plateau beyond. In the same year as Hassenein Bey's epic journey, Ball went with Prince Hussein Kemal el Din on one of the first great motorised expeditions. A new era of desert exploration had begun.

Ball found that the motor car was a boon for surveying in dune country, even though the dunes themselves posed one of the most formidable obstacles to their movement. As he explained:

Figure 27. The Little Doctor, John Ball.

Dunes are the most difficult of all desert features to map properly by ordinary reconnaissance methods with camel transport. Their smooth outlines provide no points on which intersections can be made, and no survey marks put on them will remain in place for more than a few hours, or at most a few days; they occur mostly in nearly level country, where it is impossible to find a station whence they can be overlooked; the absence of shadows on them renders it impossible to say whether one is looking at a single line of dunes, or at several lines, miles apart, one behind the other in echelon. (Ball 1927, 212).

Ball found that the only sure way of mapping dunes was to traverse their sides along their entire length, something that was impracticable with camels owing to the enormous distances which would have to be covered without water. But with motor cars Ball found that one could run alongside them at 40 km an hour instead of the camel's four, and their distribution could thus be rapidly and easily ascertained.

Ball was a dedicated surveyor and achieved much in the face of indifference from the bureaucrats from Cairo. As C.S. Jarvis, his travelling companion with Prince Kemal el Din, remarked:

> Surveying a waterless desert under any conditions is not an easy task, but what makes the feat a definite accomplishment is the fact that the Egyptian Government themselves did not care whether the wastes were mapped or not. Ball and his small following succeeding in carrying out the work despite the Government indifference and not at its instigation or with its help. This was one of the queer anomalies of service in Egypt – one found oneself working desperately hard to accomplish some particular job of work and derived encouragement and enjoyment from the knowledge that, so far from giving satisfaction to one's employers, one was actually annoying them! Until one has tried it, it is impossible to realize what an inciting and impelling force this is. (Jarvis 1938, 86).

Ball was "game to the last ounce and fit for anything". Jarvis recounted that it never mattered one jot to Ball if the cars were hopelessly stuck in the sand and extraction seemed impossible, neither did he worry if water and food were running low and death from thirst seemed a possibility. Mundane matters like this were of no concern whatsoever to Ball but it was a very different state of affairs if anything happened to the car containing his instruments or if, when one was driving him, one changed direction so suddenly that he was unable to get his speedometer reading and bearing. The very placid little man on these occasions "turned into a very good imitation of a tiger to whose posterior a red hot iron has been applied". He was also fanatical about the need for accuracy in mapping:

> Ball is a most tolerant man; he can bear with equanimity all sorts of failings and peccadilloes on the part of his friends or his enemies, if he possesses any,

but he draws the line very firmly at bad mapping. A man who goes out into the desert in a car and does some slipshod work with a pocket compass and an uncertain speedometer and then puts the result on a map as a correct reading has in his opinion committed, not one of the Seven Deadly Sins, but the deadliest sin that any man can commit. (Ibid., 87).

On some occasions this fanaticism caused friction. On the expedition with Prince Kemal el Din, Jarvis records (Ibid., 89) that he drove Ball in his car the whole time. It was fitted with a compass and a reliable speedometer, and as they went along Ball jotted down the various distances run on every bearing. The trouble was that Ball frequently desired to stop to take a few compass shots on conspicuous hills at a moment when it was impossible for Jarvis to do so owing to the presence of soft sand. Jarvis knew that a car travelling at 65 kph will skim over such sand in a delightful fashion; at 50 kph the tyres will break through the crust slightly and the engine will knock, and at 30 kph the wheels will sink right in and the car will stop. The motto for drivers was, "keep her running at all costs", as once one stopped it took a terrific amount of pushing and heart-breaking toil to get the vehicle fast enough to skim along the crust again. It was therefore very difficult to unite the two ambitions: Jarvis's desire to keep travelling at speed, and Ball's desire to get out at the critical moment and take a shot at some particular hill. As a result, tempers sometimes got very short on these desert car journeys, and after one of these occurrences, where it had been impossible to reconcile the two schools of thought, Ball and Jarvis frequently drove for hours without speaking. It was remarkable, however, how mellow they both became at the witching hour of 6pm when, with cars parked and the camp made, the whisky bottle was passed round after a tiring and nerve-racking day.

Jarvis believed (Ibid., 87) that as a rule, surveyors are filled with the same sort of proselytizing zeal that causes missionaries to end up in stew pots.

Claud Williams was also struck by the Little Doctor's zeal:

THE LITTLE DOCTOR: JOHN BALL

Precision in his observations and calculations was almost a mania with him and the fact that the position of Matruh was in doubt by some few hundred yards almost approached to a calamity in his mind. (Williams undated, 46).

Williams also lost sleep because of Ball's insatiable desire to make nocturnal star sightings and to receive midnight wireless signals from Berlin. Ball produced a book for officers so that they could undertake these tasks themselves (Ball 1917).

Ball who received the RGS's Victoria Medal in 1926, retired in 1932, and died at Port Said in 1941. He had served in the Survey of Egypt for 43 years. He was buried in the Protestant cemetery in Cairo and his tombstone inscription appropriately reads, "I will even make a way in the wilderness". Ball's obituary in the *Geographical Journal* paid tribute to his unbounded energy in the field, and remarked that "A relentless critic of his own work and other people's work, he had an uncanny knack of laying a finger on the weak spot of an argument, method or instrument." His most cherished maxim was "never miss an opportunity of making a check" (Anon 1941).

The Desert Surveys

The Government of Egypt established the Desert Surveys Department in 1920, with the specific aim of mapping areas such as the Sinai and the Western and Eastern Deserts, which, unlike the Nile valley, were hitherto largely unmapped. Ball was its first Director. The department lasted until 1937, when it was amalgamated with the Topographical Survey. From 1926 to 1931 the staff of the Desert Surveys was much involved with the discovery and mapping of the Qattara Depression, a huge depression greater in extent than Wales, and with ascertaining its potential for hydroelectric power generation were it to be linked to the Mediterranean by means of a tunnel. Ball, who named the depression after an insignificant salt spring issuing on its northern margin, thought that the fall of water into the depression could generate a great deal of electricity but the idea was abandoned as prohibitively expensive in 1931. Before that, however, the depression had been mapped in great detail with 5 m contours and lines of levels had been run from it to the Mediterranean – a distance of only about 50 km. Much of this work was undertaken by Walpole, a surveyor in the Egyptian Survey Department.

In 1931 parties of the Desert Survey reconnoitred practicable motor routes from Egypt to the Sudan on both sides of the Nile and westwards a triangulation to Gebel Uweinat, while in 1932 a triangulation pushed due west from Ain Dalla to the western frontier with Cyrenaica through the Great Sand Sea. This was the task of P.A. Clayton, whom Ball had appointed in 1923 (figure 28).

In 1932, on the retirement of Ball, G.W. Murray took over the directorship of the Desert Survey but the next few years were lean ones because of financial crisis. Indeed in the season of 1934-5, the annual budget for fieldwork was cut down to a mere pittance – £47 – and the order was actually signed for its dissolution. After the amalgamation of the Desert and Topographical Surveys in 1937, mapping was able to

Figure 28. Captain Pat Clayton at Zamalek, 1941.

continue and in 1938, 187 permanent beacons, some of them in the Great Sand Sea, were installed to mark the frontier between Libya and Egypt along meridian twenty-five (Murray 1967, 174).

In 1926 Ball's Desert Surveys Department (figure 29) bought Fords for three of its surveyors, Mr Murray, Mr Clayton and Mr Walpole. All three received the RGS's Founder's Medal: Murray in 1936, Clayton in 1941 and Walpole in 1950. Likewise, Mr and Mrs Beadnell used Model T Fords from 1927 to 1929 when they were involved with the drilling of water wells at Bir el Sahra and Bir el Messaha in the south of the desert. H.J.L. Beadnell (1874-1944) had been educated at Cheltenham College, a school that had a reputation for producing military men, rather than trying to emulate Cheltenham Ladies' College, which concentrated on more intellectual training for young females. Three of its alumni named,

Figure 29. The Desert Survey staff, Giza, 1925. In the front row, starting from the left, are Pat Clayton, George Murray, John Ball, W.F. Hume, H.L. Beadnell, O.H. Little, Hassan Sadek and George Walpole.

coincidentally, Blood, Gore and Slaughter, were to be casualties of the trenches in the First World War (Colonel Kenneth Mason, personal communication). Beadnell, after training, like Ball, at the Royal School of Mines in London, had joined the Geological Survey of Egypt in 1896, and one of his tasks had been to develop the artesian water resources of the Kharga oasis. He served in the Egyptian Expeditionary Force from 1916 to 1919, but he never attained the Directorship of the Geological Survey, which he craved (Vivian 2000). The well-digging activities of the Beadnells were remarkable. Bir el Messaha lies some 500 km from the closest human habitation some 30 km to the north of the Egypt-Sudan border. The Hungarian Count Almásy explained the reason for the Beadnells' exertions in this isolated spot in 1927. It was to test the artesian water theory of Dr Ball, who, comparing the altitude of the known oases above sea level, had drawn a map of the 'permanent water levels'. Oases were only to be found where these levels meet the surface. Where the altitude of the country is above this level, exactly the difference needs to be dug to find water. According to this theory, at Bir el Messaha, the water level lay 70 m below the surface. Beadnell, using his surveying tools, searched the area for a depression which is impossible to detect with the naked eye in the endless plain, and started his work at a point where only a shallow layer of sand covered the Nubian sandstone bedrock below:

> With the help of a handful of natives, using only the most primitive tools and plenty of explosives, they opened the well shaft in the rock. In the two square metre floor of the shaft only one person could work at a time. Day by day they carved the hole in the rock, and lifted the debris after explosions in a bucket. The cars supplied the small party with water and food from Kharga, and the indefatigable Beadnell found plenty of time during his 12-month long monotonous task to survey and map the surrounding untraversed desert in all directions.

> Exactly on Christmas Eve – at a depth of 65 meters – water was finally found. It was sweet and plentiful, exactly as Dr Ball predicted. (Almásy 1934, 37).

The two years of sand, dust and personal effort at the wells imposed a severe strain on Beadnell's health, and precluded further fieldwork (Sandford 1944). In 1931 the RGS awarded him the Cuthbert Peek Award.

At the end of 1932 the Desert Surveys Department, with Clayton as leader, made a major attack on the Great Sand Sea. Clayton's task, with his crew of drivers Abu Fudail, Manufli, and Mohammed Eid and survey men Obaid, Hassan Eid, and Hassan Shahine (who had worked with him for ten years), was the first direct east-to-west traverse across the dunes of the Great Sea of Sand along the 27th North Latitude, to the Libyan Frontier. On the plain west of the Sands a survey cairn 1.5 m high and visible for a great distance was built. This is Big Cairn on the map today (figure 30). The second leg of this expedition was to go due south near the 24th meridian through the Sand Sea to locate the northern parts of the Gilf Kebir plateau. Again, a nearly straight line, but it was along the grain of the dunes this time.

Figure 30. Big Cairn, built December 1932, on the west side of the Great Sand Sea.

On 29 December, before reaching the Gilf, they discovered deposits of silica glass on the open streets between the dunes. They went on to locate the northern edge of the Gilf and into the wooded wadi seen from the air, now known as Wadi Abd el Malik, and to Wadi Hamra to its east. In the Second World War Big Cairn was to be the start of various operational routes into Libya.

More immediately, the Libyan Desert Glass (as it is generally known) caused considerable interest and was itself the subject of The Silica Glass Research Expedition of November 1934. On that expedition Major Clayton took Dr L.J. Spencer from the British Museum and Tip (O.H.) Little.

Libyan Desert Glass was found on windswept interdune corridors formed of Cretaceous Nubian sandstone. It consists of fragments of a translucent, pale yellow-green, glassy substance, which are scattered over 6,500 km^2 of desert surface and range in size up to that of a football and with weights up to 25 kg. This beautiful natural glass, which is rather pure silica (*c.* 96.5-99% by weight) was prized by Aterian people, round about 30,000 to 40,000 years ago, for making exquisite stone tools. It was also valued by the boy king, Tutankhamun, who besides having huge holes pierced in his ears for earrings, also wore a scarab necklace made of Libyan Desert Glass. The glass is, however, much older than this, and in recent years it has been dated by a technique called fission-track analysis to around 28.5 million years old. In addition to its purity, the glass is notable for the very high temperature – c. 1,700° C – at which it begins to melt. How did it form?

Clayton believed it had an impact origin, and this is now the generally held view. In other words it is thought that the glass was formed by the impact of a meteorite or other extra-terrestrial body onto the desert surface. This shattered and fused the sandstone. Such impact glasses are called *tektites*, from the Greek *tektos*, meaning molten. However, it is only in the last few years that, using satellite images, scientists have located some of the huge craters that indicate that impacts did in fact occur in the area.

George William Murray (1885-1966) was another key figure in the exploration of the desert. A Scotsman from Aberdeen, he joined the Survey of Egypt in 1907, succeeded Ball as Director of Desert Surveys in 1932-1937, and became director of the Topographical Survey between 1937 and 1947. He played a major role in the late 1920s in surveying the newly discovered Qattara Depression and the country between the Depression and the Mediterranean. It was in this region that some of the fiercest of battles between the British Eighth Army and Erwin Rommel's *Panzerarmee* would occur.

Murray, 'Desert Murray', a friend of Freya Stark, the intrepid female explorer, and a lover of the desert, participated in several desert expeditions with his wife Edith and two large Airedale terriers. Murray himself was of very substantial size and stood in marked contrast to the diminutive Ball. There is a splendid photo of him in the frontispiece of his autobiography *Dare Me to the Desert*, with voluminous shorts and, horror of horrors, calf-length dark socks. During the Second World War, the maps of Murray and his colleagues were to prove to be of inestimable value to Bagnold.

Bagnold regarded Murray and his wife as "close and lasting friends". They enjoyed mountaineering together. Murray was awarded the RGS Founders' Medal in 1936 (Bagnold 1966).

There are doubtless other unacclaimed explorers who contributed to the many journeys described so far, but for whom we now have little information. For example, Jarvis recalls the role of a subaltern of the Frontiers Camel Corps called Fairman (Jarvis 1936, 107) in the expedition he undertook with Prince Kemal el Din. A Mr Fairman also assisted Pat Clayton in 1926 (Clayton 1998, 20). One assumes it is the same person. If so, according to Jarvis he was a hugely capable and hefty individual, over six feet (1.82 m) tall and weighing more than 14 stone (90 kg). Inevitably, he was called 'Baby'. Records show that a Sydney Maurice Fairman, formerly of the Royal Welsh (Welch) Fusiliers, served in the Imperial Camel Corps in Palestine. Perhaps it was him.

Cape to Cairo

One of the great challenges after the Great War was to drive for the first time along the great imperial swathe of Africa, proudly marked in pink on every atlas, between the Cape of Good Hope and Cairo. This had been attempted in 1913-14 by Captain Kelsey, but he only got as far as Rhodesia, where he was fatally mauled by a leopard. The journey was plainly a difficult one (Anon 1925, 246).

Captain R. Kelsey, with five other Europeans, drove from Cape to Bulawayo with little difficulty. Then their troubles began. The road to Wankie broke the driver's heart and Captain Wilson of Bulawayo took his place. The rains struck them in earnest at Broken Hill. Discarding mudguards and shedding members of the party, the rest went on until, near Chitambo, Captain Kelsey was attacked by a leopard which he had wounded. Then occurred what Captain Wilson describes as "the bravest deed I ever heard of." A native 'boy', with not even a stick in his hands, ran up, and seizing the leopard by the tail hauled it off Captain Kelsey, who then managed to reload the rifle and shoot the beast while the boy still held on to its tail. Some days later a doctor from the Chitambo mission reached him and amputated Captain Kelsey's leg there and then in the veld. Unfortunately he died while the operation was going on. Thus ended the first attempt to cross Africa by motor car. Not deterred by this tragic tale, in the 1920s a young English couple – the Court Treatts (figure 31) – decided they would have a go at the Cape to Cairo route. Chaplin Court Treatt, known to all and sundry as 'C.T.', had served in the Royal Flying Corps (RFC) in the war and had been badly smashed when the aircraft in which he was observer, was shot down. Thereafter he spent the rest of the war in Egypt. After the end of hostilities he was engaged in the building of aerodromes for the Trans-Africa Air Route. He developed the dream of driving across Africa, northwards from Cape Town, and enthused his young wife, Stella, with this ideal.

Figure 31. The Court Treatts.

While in the RFC and while working on the Trans-African Air Route, C.T. had experience of using Crossley motor cars and a pair of these was his choice for the long journey north. The Crossley is now a defunct breed that was first built in Manchester, England, in 1904. Manchester was also the English home of the Ford Model T. During its short history (production ceased in 1937) the Crossley company produced some distinguished cars. Their pre-1914 4-litre 20/25 was used by the RFC and became the first vehicle used by the Metropolitan Police Flying Squad. A derivation of it, the 4.5 litre 25/30, enjoyed royal patronage, and was supplied to no less a clientele than the Prince of Wales, the Kings of Spain and Siam, and Emperor Hirohito of Japan. It was the 25/30, with a truck body, that was used by the Court Treatts. The journey started in Cape Town in September 1924 and ended in Cairo in January 1926. The tall, pipe-smoking Major made a striking contrast to his small, tomboy wife. The last part of the journey involved a journey from Wadi Halfa up to Cairo. They decided not to use the Darb al Arba'in road, because of its deep and heavy sand. Instead they decided to go along the eastern side of the Nile from Wadi Halfa to Shellal. The problem with his route was that it was rocky and mountainous. No one thought they could get through.

In the event the journey was a frustrating one, not least for their dog Kima.

January 11 – A perfectly beastly day. We only made twenty miles. Had tyre trouble again....We seem to do nothing but twist about mountains, then go back on our own spoor [track].

Kima got away this morning while we were mending a tyre. I chased him up hills and down again, and finally caught him, when C.T. got behind a big rock and made fearsome noises like infuriated buffaloes. He was terrified and dashed for the safety of his 'mother's' arms! He loathes the desert; it seems to frighten him. He kicks and screams when I attempt to lead him from the cars. I suppose he misses the trees and grass....

To-day the guides tell us that they are quite definitely lost. We know in which direction the river lies, and if the worst happens we can make for that on foot, but it would break our hearts to abandon the cars. We cannot have come so far to lose – now! We shall have to have water soon. It is almost done. I wonder if we shall reach the Nile? If all else fails, we must attempt the desert still further east, to the Red Sea. If we must try this it will be a desperate gamble, for large tracts of it are unknown, and may be soft sand. (Court Treatt 1927, 237).

In due course they made it to Luxor where they had a wonderful stay and a splendid departure to Cairo. En route they enjoyed the pleasures of the desert:

We are camped in the desert again to-night, where all is peace. I love it so. Perhaps as much as all the lovely forest country and glorious grass-lands of Africa. So much has been said about the lure of the desert. It has an indefinable charm, the memory of which must remain always. (Ibid.).

Stella wrote a gripping and diverting account of the journey that appeared in 1927. A film was also produced.

Besides the Court Treatts, another intrepid couple made the journey across Africa. In 1923 the Renault Company of France developed cars that proved to be well suited to desert travel. These were large six-wheeled vehicles with double tyres that posed stiff competition for the caterpillar trucks of the rival Citroën firm. Between November 1924 and July 1925 Capitaine Delingette and his wife made the journey in the reverse direction to the Court Treatts, travelling from Colomb Béchar in Algeria to the Cape of Good Hope.

Zerzura and Cambyses

One of the driving forces for exploration of the Libyan Desert, which occupied and intrigued many of the travellers, was the search for the lost oasis of Zerzura. Almost all the people discussed in this book had this to a greater to lesser extent as an aim, and the story of the quest for Zerzura has been graphically described in recent years by Saul Kelly (2002) and by Théodore Monod and Edmond Diemer (2000).

The search proved to be fruitless, partly because there were so many possible locations where such an oasis might occur. The evidence to go upon was slight, involved a great deal of hearsay and generated a huge amount of debate, sometimes heated, between such figures as Colonel de Lancey Forth, Almásy, Ball, Wingate, Newbold, Harding King, Beadnell and the like. Over a period of years it occupied many pages of the *Geographical Journal*. Nowell Barnard de Lancey Forth, an Australian by birth and an ancestor of Rupert Murdoch, the newspaper proprietor, had been seconded to the Egyptian Army in 1907, and saw a great deal of service in various parts of the Sudan, during the course of which he was awarded the Military Cross. In 1917 he was appointed commander of the 3rd Battalion of the Imperial Camel Corps, and fought the Turks in Sinai and Palestine. A great admirer of Rosita Forbes, from 1920 to 1924 he was employed by the Egyptian Government as commander of the Camel Corps and Light Car Patrols. During that time he sought Zerzura (unsuccessfully) on camel treks conducted between Siwa, Ammonite Hill and Regenfeld. In 1924 he contracted an illness which for many years made him an invalid, and so his exploring career was cut short. Never a great exponent of the motor car for exploration, he died in Egypt in 1933. His obituary in the *Geographical Journal* remarked that he was:

One of those men of whom the public hears little, since their work lies on the fringe of civilization and they are not given to advertisement, but who from long experience, and a natural aptitude for their work, are able to outwit the wild native tribesmen with whom they have to deal and to beat them on their own ground. (King 1933).

Almásy and his colleagues sought Zerzura in the Gilf Kebir region, Orde Wingate sought it in the Sand Sea near Ain Dalla, and Ball thought on geological grounds it could be near Bir Terfawi, but also concluded (Ball 1928 255) that "the 'lost' oasis of Zerzura has no more real existence that the philosopher's stone". People could not even agree on the meaning of the word itself. To some it was the 'water depot of the Blacks', to others 'the oasis where pots are made', and to others 'the oasis of little birds'.

Zerzura was never conclusively found, but its appeal was enormous. As Bagnold remarked:

The possibility that there may be still in the world an undiscovered place makes an interestingly wide appeal to the civilised imagination; and when, in the pursuit of its whereabouts, one is led, owing the blankness of modern knowledge about the country in which it is supposed to lie, to search back and back, from native statements to native tradition, thence to old Arabic writings perhaps even to the Greek classics, the thing becomes as intriguing as a detective story. (Bagnold 1935, 268).

That said, Bagnold believed that it was the wadis of the Gilf Kebir that were behind the legend, and he fully acknowledged the role of Almásy in formulating this view (Bagnold 1937).

The second story that encouraged some searches, all abortive, was that of Cambyses. According to the Ancient Greek historian, Herodotus, in 525 BC, the Persian Emperor, Cambyses, hearing of the riches of the Temple of Jupiter Ammon at Siwa, detached an army of 50,000 Persians to march to Siwa by way of the Great Oasis (Kharga). The army entered the Great Sand Sea but, the story has it, a sandstorm arose and annihilated them.

Somewhere in that great waste of sand, therefore was the prospect of finding their bones, swords and armour (Wingate 1934, 281). Cambyses himself did not accompany the army into the Great Sand. He was too busy conducting an equally ill-judged campaign against Ethiopia. Nor did he last long. A self-inflicted dagger wound went gangrenous and he died, much reviled, in 522 BC.

ORDE WINGATE

One of the most famous seekers after Zerzura was a man who would later die in the steamy jungles of Assam. This was Orde Wingate (1903-44) (figure 32). He was born in India to a family that had a history of involvement with the Bible, the Sword and the East. His parents were Plymouth Brethren and he was brought up in a strictly puritan household. He was educated at Charterhouse (the public school in Surrey) and the Royal Military Academy at Woolwich before gaining a commission in the Royal Artillery in 1923. Notwithstanding signs of standard military interests – swimming, boxing, shooting and horsemanship – he began to learn Arabic at the School of Oriental Studies in London.

He was persuaded in this endeavour by his father's cousin, Sir Reginald Wingate, who had been responsible for establishing the Egyptian Frontiers Administration – in which one of the first officers was Major Jarvis, who, as we have seen, was a pioneer of desert motoring. In 1927 Wingate cycled to Brindisi in south-east Italy, sold the bike, used the proceeds to get a passage on an Italian vessel to Port Sudan, and then obtained an appointment for five years in the Sudan Defence Force. It was in 1933 that he made a five-week expedition into the Libyan Desert. This was by no means a success, but it was notable for the fact that at a time when motor expeditions were becoming the norm, he chose to go on foot, with camels being used to carry his kit.

Sir Reginald, who had been in correspondence with Count Almásy and his Austrian colleague, Dr Richard Bermann, made some effort to persuade Wingate to join the Almásy-Bermann motor expedition. Wingate, however, was bent on travelling alone and by camel. He went to Dakhla by motor lorry and met up with his thirteen ill-trained camels and four Arab cameleers. Then he travelled with them to Bir Abu Mungar before heading westwards in the direction of Kufra along the old track. Half way through the expedition he found, not Zerzura, but the car of

Figure 32. Orde Wingate in 1943.

Pat Clayton of the Desert Survey Department. As Christopher Sykes observed:

> There are many perils and terrors, and hideous discomfort, in explorations such as those of Doughty and Burton in whose footsteps Wingate was piously and humbly treading, but the worst calamity of all is to find at the end of an agonising march of two weeks that the whole road can be done in a day by a car. (Sykes 1959, 80).

Subsequently Orde Wingate became a Zionist, helped to liberate Ethiopia from the Italian yoke and to reinstate Emperor Haile Selassie. Exhausted by his efforts and tribulations in that theatre, he attempted suicide by trying to cut his own throat and spent some months in hospital. One of his military colleagues, Hugh Boustead, who was also a traveller in the Western Desert, and who disliked Wingate, visited him in hospital and said to him, "You bloody fool, why didn't you use a revolver?" (Thesiger 1987, 353). Here, however, we have yet another link with the Western Desert, for General Archbiald Wavell, from August 1939 Commander-in-Chief of the newly created Middle East Command, under whom he had served briefly in Palestine, was the person who decided that Wingate should undertake that role in East Africa. It was also Wavell who was to allow Bagnold to set up the LRDG and it was Wavell and Wingate who set up a 'Long Range Penetration Group' (the Chindits) to operate behind Japanese lines in the reconquest of Burma. During the Burma campaign Major-General Wingate, as he had become, was killed when his aircraft crashed into the Naga jngles of north Assam during a tropical storm. Hence died a man noted for his genius, "his insubordination, ruthless ambition, calculated rudeness and emotional instability." (Dear and Foot 2001, 997).

BAGNOLD

After the First World War some of the Duke of Westminster's men and machines were transferred to the 3rd Armoured Car Company. Among the men was Lieutenant A.J. Bather, who was stationed at Sollum on the frontier between Italian and British territory. It was Bather, on his recall to Cairo in 1924, who first started the idea that so intrigued Ralph Bagnold (figure 33) and his colleagues that "There was fun to be got out of a holiday in the desert, if one set about it in the right way" (Bagnold 1935, 17). As Ralph Bagnold relates, V.C. Holland and Bather spent a week over Christmas 1924 on the edge of the Western Desert:

> During that week Holland got thoroughly bitten with the whole idea of the thing; with the sense of freedom to go just where one liked, driving on a compass course; with the awe of a new utterly lifeless world; with the thrill of forcing a car at obstacles that no car was designed to encounter; with the clean coolness of sand dunes in the evening, and the dry sparkling desert air. They did the thing properly; they were away from water and so they stuck to the rules that Bather had learnt; there was a daily water ration for drinking only, there was no washing, and they went unshaved. They thoroughly enjoyed themselves. (Ibid., 18).

Bagnold was small and wiry, shy by nature, discerning and sociable with his friends, extremely practical around the house and in creating scientific instruments, and a keen climber and snooker player (Keen 1991). He was posted to Egypt for the three years from 1926-1929 and discovered that he and Holland (a school chum from his days at Malvern College) had similar tastes. Bagnold sold his little English car, bought a Ford, and with Holland started to probe westwards. Indeed, the central figure in the story of car travel in the Libyan Desert was Ralph Alger Bagnold. He was born in Devonport in the west of England in 1896, the second child

Figure 33. Ralph Bagnold.

of an officer in the Royal Engineers who had himself served in Egyptian and the Sudan. His sister was Enid Bagnold, the author and lover of that notorious sex addict, Frank Harris. His education was conventional. He started at a preparatory school in Bexhill (a seaside town in south-east England), went on to Malvern College (a minor public school of which he was not excessively fond) and then progressed to the Royal Military Academy at Woolwich as a gentleman cadet. In 1915 he joined the Royal Engineers and was sent to France as a member of the British Expeditionary Force. He fought in the bloody, muddy trenches at the Somme, Ypres and Passchendaele and was mentioned in dispatches. After the war he did the Engineering Tripos course at Cambridge University before returning to the Army in 1921. In 1926 he was posted to Egypt and it was during leave that he developed his passion for desert exploration by motor car.

After a couple of years he was sent off to the frontiers of India, but in 1931 was posted back to the far less exciting world of Catterick Garrison in the north of England. However, he was granted permission to conduct an expedition in the Western Desert, for which he was awarded the RGS's Founder's Medal in 1934. Thereafter he served in the Far East but was taken ill with 'tropical sprue' (a digestive complaint) and was discharged from the Army as 'a permanent invalid'. The gloomy diagnosis of his condition proved to be unfounded and he survived and flourished for another five and a half decades, dying on 28 May, 1990, at the age of 94.

He embarked with gusto on a new career in scientific investigation at Imperial College, London, with the aim of understanding sand movement and dune development. To this end he conducted the first experiments with a wind tunnel and in 1938 undertook further journeys deep into the Libyan Desert, visiting the Gilf Kebir, Jebel Uweinat and the Selima Sand Sea.

When the Second World War started Bagnold returned to the Army, which in its wisdom, decided to send him to Kenya, a colonial territory of which he had no previous experience. Fate was to intervene and to ensure his return to Egypt. There he used his unique experience to establish a special army unit, the LRDG, to commit "piracy on the high desert" and to harry the Italians and Rommel.

The 1929 Bagnold Expedition

In the winter of 1873-1874, Gerhard Rohlfs led a German expedition that attempted to cross the Great Sand Sea from Dakhla to Kufra. However, no expedition capable of making precise observations had penetrated this area of enormous dunes since then. The general view, shared by such leaders of motor expeditions as Prince Kemal el Din and Omar Toussoon, was that this terrain was just too difficult for motor vehicles. Bagnold was keen to test the veracity of this advice.

In November 1929 Bagnold and five colleagues secured a month's leave. Captain V.F. Craig (Royal Engineers), was in charge of food supplies and theodolite work; Captain R.G.L. Giblin (Royal Signals) was in charge of the wireless transmitter set and the collection of time signals; Lt D.W. Burridge (Royal Signals) and Lt I.B. Fernie (Royal Tank Corps) were in charge of camp arrangements; Lt G.L. Prendergast (Royal Tank Corps) and Bagnold were responsible for car maintenance and repairs.

Guy Prendergast, who like Bagnold was later to command the LRDG in World War Two, was a man of distinctive character, described by David Lloyd Owen in these terms:

> Aloof, almost to the extent of appearing stand-offish and some even found him so; shy, almost to a degree when he would avoid people who had not come to see him on business; efficient, almost to the exclusion of ever relaxing; calm, almost in that he seemed to have no emotion; intolerant, almost that he could barely understand those who were less phlegmatic, enthusiastic and bound by the same sense of duty as he was. (Lloyd Owen 1957, 80).

On the other hand, Lloyd Owen recognised that underneath a façade of the unapproachable automaton there was a generous heart and natural charm.

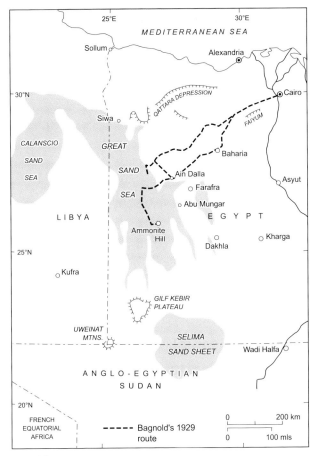

Map 7. Bagnold's 1929 journey.

Their aim was to motor south-westwards from Cairo via Gebel Misawag, Alam el Ghard, and mounts Ehrenberg and Minutoli. They then headed further south-westwards into dune country in the vicinity of Camp 9, before turning south-eastwards to Ain Dalla and thence back to Cairo. They had three vehicles – two Ford 30 cwt lorries and a touring car of the same make. The lorries proved to be too heavy for dune country, but "the Ford touring car's performance was so remarkable that by the end of the journey I was confident of getting across any dune country of the type we had met" (Bagnold 1931, 18). The car also had a low petrol consumption (5 km per litre), could carry a reasonable pay load (770 kg) and gave promise of a self-contained range of action of 1,900 km. This was the way forward.

Ain Dalla was a crucial location for those intending to voyage into the dunes, for it was a source of water. It is a small, lonely depression carved out of the desert plateau by wind, and bounded on the north and east by cliffs and to the south and west by dunes. In its centre there were tussocks of tamarisk and grass and a few straggling date palms located on a small hill. The hill is a 'spring mound' formed in the course of time by dust and sand being trapped by the spring's moisture. It had been used by the Romans, and just before Bagnold's visit the spring had been dug out and conducted into a pipe by Prince Omar Toussoon.

The great significance of the 1929 journey was that it proved that the Great Sand Sea could be penetrated by car (figure 34, map 7). It was also a journey in which navigation and mechanical skills, and the use of sand tracks were honed. Bagnold found the ability to climb sand dunes to be quite exhilarating, not least because the wall of dune had appeared so daunting:

Ahead, not far away, along the whole of the western horizon, lit up by an early morning sun, lay the golden wall of dunes. Through field-glasses their regular rows of summits could be seen. There was nothing else. The earth was dead flat, and on nearer approach to the dunes they seemed in contrast to rise up in front as mountain ranges. By noon the uppermost rampart of sand was reached, a straight line of summits running across our path. Regularly spaced crests towered up as if a giant wave were about to break. (Bagnold 1935, 127).

The dunes, however, were not unbroken, and three were areas where the dune sand proved to be unexpectedly firm. The daring Bagnold decided

Figure 34. Bagnold's 1929 expedition vehicles.

to have a go (Ibid., 128). He increased their speed to 60 kph, feeling, he said, like a small boy on a horse about to take his first big fence. He saw Burridge holding on grimly to the side of the vehicle. Suddenly the light doubled in strength as if more suns had been switched on. A huge glaring wall of yellow shot up high into the sky a yard in front of them. The lorry tipped violently backwards – and they rose as in a lift, smoothly without vibration. They floated up and up on what appeared to be a yellow cloud. All the accustomed car movements ceased; only the speedometer told them they were still moving fast. It was incredible. Instead of sticking deep in loose sand at the bottom as instinct and experience foretold, they found that were near the top a hundred feet above the ground. Bagnold cut off the engine and let the car come to a rest gently to await the others. He found the sand was covered with little ripples that had flown by too fast to be seen when the car was on the move. His wheel tracks were barely a centimetre deep and trailed out behind quite cleanly like a pair of railway lines. However, he found that the sand was quite soft. He ran his fingers through it easily, and found that there was no surface crust to support the wheels. It was just the special way the grains were packed.

Dunes could be conquered.

The 1930 Bagnold expedition

The 1929 expedition had been so instructive that in October and November 1930 Bagnold decided to attempt a far more ambitious journey (map 8), starting from a previously formed dump at Ain Dalla. The intention was to head from there across the Great Sand Sea and to make a loop back to Ain Dalla via Rohlfs' Ammonite Hill. From Ain Dalla a second run would be attempted through the Sand Sea south-west to Uweinat and thence east of Selima, where a further dump was arranged. The stretch from Ammonite Hill, around 1,700 km, was estimated to be within the self-contained range of the three Ford cars that were to be used.

The party consisted of Bagnold, D. Newbold, W.B.K. Shaw, V.C. Holland, G.L. Prendergast and D.A.L. Dwyer. Douglas Newbold appears again in our story when in the Second World War he gave advice to Bagnold about how to set about mounting an LRDG raid with the French on the Libyan town of Murzuk. Newbold (1894-1945) was born in genteel Tunbridge Wells, the youngest of a family of 11 children, attended Uppingham (a public school in the midlands county of Rutland) and then went up to Oriel College at Oxford to read Classics. That far his life was tolerably conventional. However, his Oxford career was interrupted by the First World War, in which he was commissioned in the Dorset Yeomanry and the Cavalry Machine Gun Corps. He served in Egypt and Palestine. After chasing the Sanussi he took part in cavalry charges at Agagia (between Mersa Matruh and Sollum in Egypt) and Mughar (Palestine) and was wounded at Zeitun in Palestine after the fall of Gaza in November 1917. When he returned to his Oxford studies he had already developed an interest in the Middle East and its history and archaeology. This persuaded him to join the Sudan Political Service, where he saw service in Kordofan. A lifelong bachelor, he developed a taste for desert exploration and had undertaken expeditions into the Libyan Desert., including one he made by camel in 1927 across unexplored country to Selima with W.B.K. Shaw

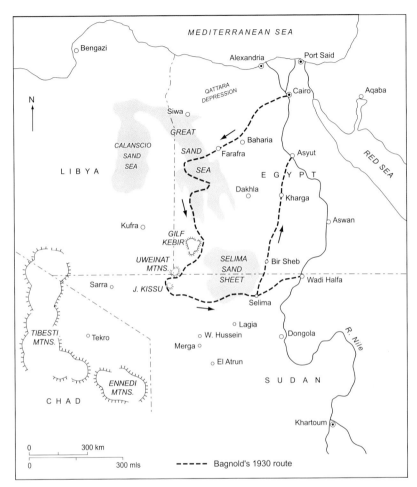

Map 8. Bagnold's 1930 journey.

(the same Shaw who joined the LRDG in 1940). He was also very protective
of the interests of the people of the Sudan who to his mind were "some of
the finest people in the world". His archaeological, anthropological and
historical interests added greatly to the knowledge of the Sudanese portions
of the Libyan Desert. He became Chief Secretary of the Government of
Sudan at the outbreak of war and so was in a position to give the LRDG

Figure 35. Bottoms up! Bagnold's 1930 expedition getting out sand tracks.

invaluable help and advice. He was knighted in 1944 but died the following year after a riding accident in Khartoum.

As for Bill Shaw (W.B. Kennedy Shaw, 1901-1979), after being educated at Radley (a public school near Oxford) and University College, Oxford, he had entered the Sudan Civil Service in 1924 as a Forestry official, but subsequently became a professional archaeologist. He took part in various excavations in the Middle East and from 1936 to 1940 worked for the then Palestine Department of Antiquities. He was described thus by Michael Mason:

> In person he is slight and well made; neither tall nor short; long legged for his height, active and very enduring; gentle in speech and by nature silent. His mind is tidy and academic. His natural abhorrence of showing his feelings leads him to acquit his own utterances of all passion by rendering the most human of them into Latin. Bill would pass unnoticed in a crowd until something happened; then without doing anything apparent, he would lead that crowd with efficiency. (Mason 1936, 19).

The expedition left Cairo on 13 October, and made for Ain Dalla, where they were able to drink the warm, artesian, slightly sulphurous water. They set out from there on 17 October and in four and a half days travelled nearly 600 km over the waves of the Sand Sea. During this journey the three light touring cars (figure 35) lost no water whatever and averaged 5.1 km per litre of petrol. The drivers gained a clear appreciation of the relationship between areas of hard going ('liquid sands') and the contours of the land and the hues of the sand. Bagnold proffered an explanation for the presence of these liquid sands:

The lack of firm packing properties is almost certainly due to the constancy of size of the grains. The firm sand of the whaleback dunes is made up of a graduation of gauge, and the finer gauges are well mixed with the coarser so that all interstices are filled and relative movement is difficult, the mass being as near solid as it can be. The liquid patches are composed of one gauge of large grains. Owing to the slight inequalities of size, perfect 'cannon ball' piling is impossible over a large volume and the result is a 'strained piling' which occupies the maximum space. Any pressure will cause a local shrinking into 'cannon ball' piling at the point where the pressure is applied, and this shrinking will make room for further movement elsewhere. Sometimes the general movement caused by stamping one's foot is so widespread that a definite quake takes place, spreading outward in a circle several yards wide. The boundary between hard and liquid sand is usually very sharp. Superficially it is quite invisible, except over a large area as a faint change of reflecting power in certain lights. Groping with one's hand however in the mobile material, the firm sand can be felt with the fingers somewhat as one feels the inside wall of a bucket of water. It is strange that the grains of very fine sand driving over the surface in a wind have not been caught by and mixed with the coarser grains as they are mixed in the firmer material. (Bagnold 1931, 22).

Bagnold plainly became smitten by the dunes of the Great Sand Sea:

We travelled in an unstable world of bare curving sand high above the rock. Strangest of all was the unnatural regularity of the dunes. They are identical in character and details of form, maintain their geometrical straightness throughout their great length, and are parallel to one another to within 2deg. We felt always in the presence of vast purposeful organisms, slowly creeping southwards through the ages, engulfing all that might have been in their way. (*The Times*, 3 January 1931).

The second part of the journey involved travelling down to Uweinat, where water was available, and then across to Selima and Wadi Halfa before taking the Darb Al Arba'in road to Kharga and Asyut. They returned to Cairo on 15 November. In 34 days they had travelled almost 5,000 km. The day's run, even in the most difficult dune country of the Great Sand Sea, never fell below around 100 km, and the average over the total number of running days was 220 km per day.

On this expedition Bagnold got his first glimpse of the unknown plateau of the Gilf Kebir. To him:

It seemed like the frontier of some 'lost world', unscaleable, at least for car or camel, unbroken except where the mouths of deep unlit gorges appeared as black slits, from the bottom of which an ancient debris of boulders spewed out fanwise for miles into the plain. (Bagnold 1935, 164).

He was also impressed by his first glimpse of Uweinat, which "looked from any direction like some colossal crumbling citadel surrounded down below by the mounds of its ruined town". Selima also had its appeal. It was then "the oasis of a story-book, uninhabited by man and rarely visited, consisting of two little clumps of green palms, carpeted beneath with grass, and a small stone ruin of uncertain date". Like Ain Dalla and Uweinat it was a vital source for water.

The fact that such distances as those covered on this expedition could be achieved safely and quickly can be put down to three devices that enabled cars to penetrate the deepest recesses of the desert, including the Great Sand Sea.

One of these was a quick and practical method to extricate bogged-down vehicles. The solution was simple (Bagnold 1990, 68). In a Cairo junk shop they found a few steel channel sections, about 1.5 m long and about 28 cm wide, which had been intended for roofing dugouts during the First World War. These were found to be the perfect answer to the sand problem. A little valley was scooped out by hand from in front of each rear wheel, sloping downward to the base of each tyre. A channel section was laid in each valley, on which the wheels could bite as the car accelerated forward. They found that this usually carried the car well beyond the front ends of the channels and onto firm sand. They discovered that the car's two occupants, working together, could complete the operation in a very short time.

The second device was one which provided an ability to navigate even over rough ground. Navigation, as distinct from map-reading, was a necessity. As Bill Shaw remarked, if you abolish rain, you remove with it most of the natural landmarks by which the inhabitant of Europe, map in hand, can find his way over the country. Much of the desert is largely featureless, for thousands of years of wind action have produced vast plains of sand and gravel over which the movement by car in any direction is not much restricted (Shaw 1943). Normal magnetic compasses were not the answer. Bagnold recognized that there was a problem with the time-honoured method of keeping track of where one is in unknown country by fixing the bearing of a distant feature ahead with a prismatic compass, going to it and checking back if possible to the point one started from and then repeating the operation for the next conspicuous point, and so on. Very often there were no conspicuous points. No less significant was the effect that magnetism of the car itself could have on a prismatic compass:

> The compass can, of course, be fixed to the car and used as a ship's compass
> by compensating with adjustable magnets for the magnetic disturbance of

the car. But a car is not like a ship or even an aeroplane. There are generally too many movable steel parts near by, such as gear levers, spare springs, etc., the shifting of whose positions may seriously affect the compensation. (Bagnold 1935, 69).

The solution to this problem was the sun compass (figure 36). Here again Bagnold displayed his ingenuity. Simply, this was a steel knitting needle set vertically in the centre of a horizontal white shadow disc three inches (7.6 cm) in diameter. The face of the disc was graduated in 360 degrees of bearing, and the disc could be rotated in its fixed mounting to follow the sun through the day from east through south to west, according to a card giving the sun's azimuth every ten minutes of the day. Since solar time was being used, the card also gave the equation of time for the calendar day. The compass was mounted on the dashboard of a car and was always exposed since the cars had neither windscreens nor rooves. The sun's shadow was always visible, even when the sky was overcast. Occasionally, around midday when the sun was directly overhead, there was no shadow, but this was not a problem as it was when they had their midday meal. He pointed out the virtues of the device and how it was actually used:

> Leaving the driver to pick his own way, and holding onto nothing but a pencil and notebook, the navigator concentrated on recording mileage and bearing. At every halt, out came the map, protractor and latitude-longitude scale, and the last bit of course was plotted. In the evening, the dead-reckoning map position was checked against the astrofix position calculated from readings taken with theodolite, chronometer, and time signals. The day's plot was rarely more than 1 percent off, even when the route had involved much wriggling between hills and sand dunes. (Bagnold 1990, 68).

Bagnold did not so much invent the sun compass as refine it. The first use of a sun compass for motor cars in the Libyan Desert

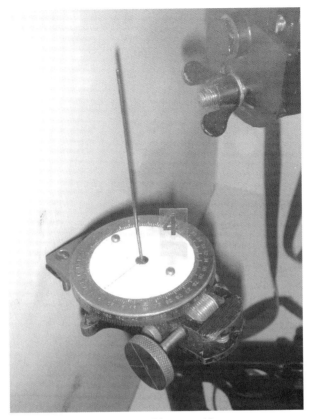

Figure 36. A sun compass of the type used by Bagnold.

(Newbold 1928, 529) was during the First World War, when it was used by the Light Car Patrols. The original model was described by John Ball in the Survey of Egypt's handbook issued in January 1917 for Military Patrols, and entitled *Desert Reconnaissance by Motor Car*. This prototype sun-compass was found to be very useful but obviously suffered from two disadvantages: (a) that halts were necessary every 8 km or so to repeat the sightings owing to the continual change in the sun's azimuth; and (b) that if stony or soft going compelled the driver to deviate from his line there was no accurate method of noting his detour.

A third device that permitted long distance travel into the desert was one that greatly reduced the use of water for cooling the cars' engines. On his trip in Sinai in 1927, the cars had boiled continuously, losing as much as 9 litres each in a day. The solution was once again simple but effective. Bagnold realised that cars do not use much water by actually boiling it off in steam, but that the steam blowing violently down the narrow overflow pipe provided in all radiators carried with it a great quantity of water splashed up by the boiling. He found that all this could be saved if the overflow were led into a special tank, even if the steam itself was lost. So he blocked up the overflows of the radiators, and in their place soldered large copper pipes to the filler-caps, joining them by other tubes down into two-gallon (9-litre) cans bolted on to the cars' running-boards, so that the only outlet from the radiator was at the end of a pipe immersed in cold water at the bottom of a can. When the water boiled in the engine a mixture of water and steam was saved, and so, until at last the water in the can itself began to boil, the steam was condensed and saved. He recognised that this solution was not entirely new, for the same idea was evolved by the Light Car Patrols during the First World War:

> The beauty of the idea is that it saves water in another way also, which we had not thought of; for by leading the connecting pipe within reach of the driver's hand, it enables him, by feeling if it is hot or cold, to tell exactly when the circulating water is starting to boil. He then turns his car round till its head points into the wind, and stops to let things cool down. After a minute or so, when the steam has condensed in the radiator top and formed a vacuum there, the water rushes back out of the can with a loud gurgle, and the radiator is full once more. (Bagnold 1935, 68).

That said, even with condensers, the cars' engines could get very hot in the summer months. They started off by being bakied from the direct rays of the sun, and then if forced to operate in low gear on soft surfaces they got fiercely hot in just a few minutes.

The cars had to be adapted so that weight was minimised and so that the risk of damage to stores due to vibration and bumping was reduced. Special bodies were constructed (Bagnold 1931, 19). Everything had to fit tightly and yet be easily off-loaded. They found that the best unit of packing was the 8-gallon (36-litre) wooden petrol case, holding two 4-gallon (18-litre) tins. The box bodies of the cars were built so that their inside measurements were a whole number of cases wide, long and high. As far as possible all stores, whether food, spare parts, tools, or petrol, were packed in these cases, which were a convenient size and weight for any handling that had to be done. The whole assemblage of cases was then held down by battens fitting over bolts rising from the outside walls of the body and pressed down by butterfly nuts. They found that this means there were no breakages or loss of petrol due to leaking tins. Water was carried in new 2-gallon (9-litre) petrol tins in rows seven a side bolted along the running-boards. Rubber washers were fitted to the stoppers instead of the usual leather ones, and no loss of water was experienced.

Tyres were another important consideration. Those fitted to the Model Ts were narrow, so that the surface to weight ratio was poor. This posed a problem where the going was soft. There were two solutions – broader tyres and lower pressures. Reducing tyre pressures on sand, so that the tyre squashed out flabbily, provided marvellous results and seemed to create no ill effects on the tyres themselves. However, alternations of hard and soft going could become tedious (Bagnold 1935, 149). With their tyres pumped hard (even harder than was recommended by the makers should the cars be grossly overloaded as theirs were), they never had any trouble in true desert country, where there are no troublesome thorns. Good tyres, they found, stood up well, without even the treads becoming worn, to any amount of scrambling over bare rocks and bouncing over stones. Similarly, in continuous sand they could be run flat for a few thousand kilometres. The difficulty began where sand alternated with rocks and stones. Here they had to run with the tyres soft over the sand to prevent the car sticking, yet had to have them hard again before a single patch of stones was encountered. In this case they found that trouble with burst tyres was a question of will power, for it was not at all easy to force themselves to stop in the hot sun at midday and pump up four tyres by hand from 10 to 40 psi (0.70-2.75 bars) pressure.

Broader tyres were also employed, particularly after the introduction of the Model A Ford. The so-called 'air wheels' were 9 inches (23 cm) wide and were excellent in soft going (see Penderel 1934).

Bagnold was also, it has to be remembered, a signals officer, and he used short-wave radios to get precise times that were so necessary for navigation and surveying. The Phillips short-wave receiver survived well, placed on the car's footboard and encased in a box that was well sprung and packed round with rubber inner tubes. They received time signals every night from the French station at Issy. They were remarkably loud and clear even in remote places like Uweinat and Wadi Halfa. The radios stood up to the bumpy conditions much better than did their chronometers, even though these were carefully packed in cotton waste in a wooden box and kept horizontal.

THE 1932 BAGNOLD EXPEDITION

In 1931 Bagnold returned to England from India to become chief instructor at the School of Signals at Catterick in Yorkshire. Life was dull. However, he happened to encounter Bill Shaw in the map room of the RGS and they hatched the idea of going on an enormous journey to visit the north-west of Sudan and the unexplored frontier regions bordering the French province of Chad. The area was in some turmoil and they would have to be self-contained for 2,400km and to travel nearly 10,000 km in all. Arms would be a necessity (map 9). It was decided to go as a party of eight in four cars – Model A Fords, which since 1927 had succeeded the Model T. The new Ford was the first made by that company which had what are now considered to be conventional controls, with normal brake and clutch pedals, throttle and gearshift. It had more gears than the Model T and could also reach higher speeds. It also had drum brakes. However, it was still cheap – $385 for a basic roadster model – and nearly 5,000,000 were produced between 1928 and 1932.

The party consisted of Bagnold, Major Hugh Boustead (Commander of the Western Camel Corps), Lt R.N. Harding-Newman (Royal Tank Corps), Bill Shaw, Dr Kenneth Sandford (a rather crusty Oxford geologist who did a great deal of valuable stone age research in Egypt), Lt Guy Prendergast, and two other young officers, Captain V.F. Craig and Lt D.R. Paterson.

Hugh Boustead (figure 37) was a particularly fascinating figure. Born on a tea estate in Ceylon in 1895, he originally was destined for the Royal Navy and received a naval education at Osborne, formerly Queen Victoria's home, on the Isle of Wight. However, by entirely irregular means during the First World War he was able to transfer to the army via a South African unit. Through this he saw service in the Western Desert against the Sanussi and the Turks. He, like so many others, endured Mersa Matruh and literally followed in the wake of the Duke of Westminster's armoured cars, lugging a 40 kg pack the 288 km from Mersa Matruh to

Figure 37. Hugh Boustead – a face "wrinkled like a walnut".

Sollum. He was awarded an MC for bravery on the Western Front, one of a range of decorations he received. After the war he went to Oxford to read Russian, gaining a place at Worcester College, where he found the Provost to be "an elderly gentleman with no contact whatsoever with the world as I knew it". He spent much of his time boxing, and competed in the modern pentathlon at the 1920 Antwerp Olympic Games. In 1924 he returned to Egypt and was appointed to the Sudan Defence Force and to the Camel Corps. In time he got to know and admire Douglas Newbold, who recommended him to Bagnold as suitable material for the 1932 expedition. In 1933, this remarkable man was a member of the RGS's Mount Everest Expedition. In the Second World War he worked with another Western Desert traveller, Orde Wingate, in the Ethiopian campaign, though their relationship was far from cordial. Later in his career he became a hugely eccentric and very grand British colonial figure in the Middle East, serving in Arabia, and noted for having a face that was latterly "wrinkled like a walnut". He was a bachelor of shortish stature who spent his final years in the United Arab Emirates, where, until he died in Dubai in 1980, he looked after the horses of the ruler, Sheik Zaid bin Sultan in a large stables in al-Ain. A rich life indeed.

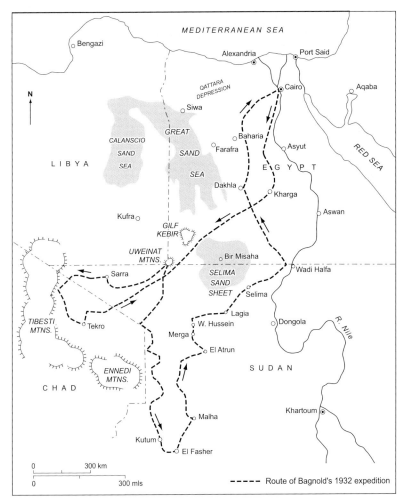

Map 9. Bagnold's 1932 journey.

Rupert Harding-Newman, who died in October 2007, in his hundredth year, had been educated at St Edward's School ('Teddy's') in Oxford before being commissioned into the Royal Tank Corps in 1928. He was sent to Egypt, and used any excuse to get out into the desert to try out new vehicles – Rileys, Jowetts and Crossleys. In the spring of 1931 he drove an

Figure 38. An Italian patrol.

Austin Seven overland back to Bovington in England (obituary in the *Daily Telegraph*, 11 December 2007). He remained with tanks for most of his army career, and before he retired in 1961 he had commanded the Royal Armoured Corps Centre at Bovington in Dorset, as well as being an ADC to the Queen. In 1942, when Brigadier Major of the 22nd Armoured Brigade, he received the Military Cross for his gallantry in fierce fighting near Hagrag el Raml.

The first objective of the expedition was to reach Uweinat, the meeting point of the Egyptian and Libyan frontiers and Sudan. It was an area of some political sensitivity and there was also the possibility of meeting armed raiders. Uweinat was to be the base where large stores of petrol and food could be dumped at Kissu for a 1,900 km journey westward into the Sarra triangle (a tongue of the then Sudanese territory which juts out westwards towards the Tibesti Mountains and was ceded to Italy in 1934) and for a 2,200 km journey southwards to the Sudanese settlement of El Fasher. Uweinat was supplied by dashing across the Selima Sand Sheet to Selima itself. On one occasion the 480 km journey was accomplished with fully laden cars in one day of less than 11 hours. While at Uweinat the Bagnold party scaled the summit ("an arduous and very thirsty scramble") and explored the volcanic craters between Uweinat and the Gilf Kebir, craters that the earlier Almásy-Clayton expedition had seen from the air. At Uweinat they encountered a detachment of Italian troops (figure 38) commanded by Major Ottavio Rolle, Governor of Kufra. The meeting was cordial.

The expedition duly set off for the Sarra triangle, visiting Sarra and Tekro. At the wells of Sarra they met another Italian troop under the command of the luxuriantly bearded Major Orlando Lorenzini. Lorenzini, who had played a part in the suppression of the Sanussi, was a desert enthusiast who impressed Bagnold. Over a sumptuous meal, provided by the Italians, Lorenzini raised a question that was to haunt Bagnold in 1940.

The question was simple, "the Nile at Aswan is only nine hundred miles from Uweinat. If there is a war, what fun it would be to take a battalion to Aswan and seize the dam [the original one completed in 1902]. What could you do?" The Sarra journey was to have further war-time significance when the French from Chad and the LRDG were to attack Italian forces at Kufra.

The second part of the expedition involved a journey from Uweinat southwards to El Fasher and then back northwards from there to Cairo via Wadi Halfa.

All in all this was both a lengthy, cheap and successful trip. As Bagnold was to relate:

The whole journey totalled over 6,000 miles, including the two runs from Kissu to Selima and back. Of this distance more that 5,000 miles was over country with no existing tracks. Much of it was very bad going for cars,

Figure 39. The Bagnold Team (1932).

being covered either with large stones and boulders, or, in the south, with hidden water runnels of hard mud. Apart from the cracking of one of the main engine-supporting brackets, which occurred within sight of the Tibesti Mountains and which was partly responsible for our decision not to go farther west, no serious fault occurred to any of the four cars, which at times were twisted and bumped about unmercifully. (Bagnold 1933, 120).

Bagnold said that it often astonished people when he told them that the gross cost per member of this type of expedition worked out at about £20-30 per 1,000 miles (1,600 km), without allowing for any rebates, such as the proceeds of the sale of the cars afterwards.

The speed of the whole expedition was also remarkable. The team (figure 39) left Cairo on 27 September 1932 and arrived back there on 29 November. It was entirely appropriate that in 1934, the RGS, which had supported the 1929, 1930 and 1932 expeditions, should have awarded Bagnold its Gold Medal for all he had accomplished to date in the Libyan Desert.

One of the people who gave financial support to Bagnold for the 1932 expedition was Mrs Patrick Ness (figure 40) (Ibid.,104). She herself had

Figure 40. Mrs Patrick Ness.

Figure 41. Gertrude Caton Thompson.

been travelling in Africa since 1906 and was the first woman elected to the Council of the then staunchly reactionary RGS. She took interest in Bagnold's exploits probably because she herself was a determined desert motorist. She drove to Lake Chad in a second-hand Morris, went across the Sahara (Tiltman 1935) in a French commercial vehicle, and in 1923 made one of the earliest car journeys from Beirut to Baghdad in a convoy of American Buicks. In 1953 she endowed the RGS's Mrs Patrick Ness Award. She died on 22 April 1962.

Her obituary makes it clear that she was an exceptional individual:

> At a time when the age of envy is superseding the age of deference, she expected deference, and her unshakable integrity and unusual beauty entitled her to it. She looked like an aristocrat of the French Revolution. Even the animals were impressed by her dignity. Once when she walking alone in what were then the untrodden wilds of Kenya, she found herself looking into the eyes of a lioness. On being asked afterwards what happened next, she replied: "She fled." (*The Times*, 3 May 1962).

Other ladies were also involved in motoring in the desert, including the great archaeologist, Gertrude Caton Thompson (figure 41), who used Fords to survey Fayum and elsewhere with her companion Elinor Gardner. Gertrude, who died aged 97, was privately educated, the daughter of a stockbroker, and never held a professional post in a museum or a university. Described in her *Times* obituary of 25 April 1985, as quiet, private and retiring, she was also said to be intrepid and absolutely indomitable in her pioneering field-work. Many men were terrified of her. It is said that while working at Abydos she slept in an emptied tomb with cobras for company and a pistol under her pillow to ward off prowling hyenas.

The 1938 Bagnold Expedition

In 1938 Bagnold decided that he needed to validate the work he had been doing on sand movement processes in his wind tunnel against real world conditions. Once more, with the help of the RGS, he returned to the desert accompanied by archaeologists and surveyors. The journey (map 10) took them to Uweinat, the Gilf Kebir and the Selima Sand Sea. Most of the time Bagnold's fieldwork involved waiting for a sand storm to occur so that he could witness and measure sand grains in action, but he also wanted to do "a bit of long-needed exploration." His objective was to drive on to the top of the Gilf Kebir. Its cliffs had deterred this ambition in the past. Bagnold and Peel managed to find a way up (Bagnold 1990, 115). Their expedition reached the Gilf cliffs early in February 1938 and they camped halfway along its eastern side. The archaeologists started about their business, while Bagnold and Ronald Peel, in a single car, drove north along the foot of the Gilf, farther than anyone had previously ventured. They came to a huge solitary sand drift that had spilled over from the plateau until its upper edge was level with the top. The sand surface was surprisingly firm as they walked up its crest. They also noticed a few rocks on it that were far too big to have been put there by the wind and realised that someone must have dropped them long ago. On their fourth attempt they succeeded in getting the car up the crest of the drift. They were then on the hard rock of the plateau itself. To them it seemed that they had strayed into a secret Stone Age world. The top of their sand drift was signposted by a pair of tall cairns, that had plainly been neatly built by a professional. Their drift must have provided the only access long ago, just as it did now. A well-worn path led inland from the brink of the plateau to successive factories of stone tools. Debris from their manufacture lay strewn everywhere and looked so fresh they half expected to come upon "a group of uncouth artisans round the next corner". Yet they found no scrap of evidence that anyone had been here since prehistoric times.

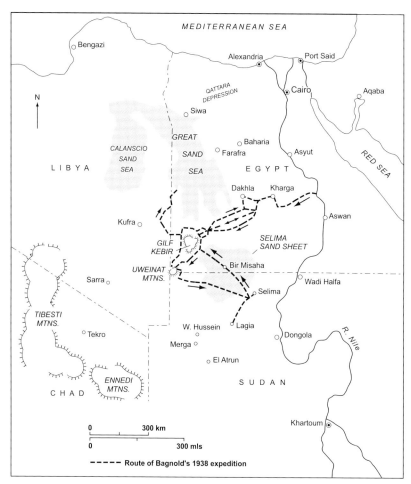

Map 10. Bagnold's 1938 journey.

The Sandstone Plateau of the Gilf Kebir, only discovered in 1926, was the subject of detailed scientific scrutiny during the 1938 expedition by Bagnold and Peel. The plateau was described by Peel:

This plateau...has a total length north to south of about 150 miles, a maximum breadth of some 50 miles, and a total area about equal to that

130

of Wales. On all sides except the north it is sharply separated from the surrounding plains by abrupt cliffs, having average slopes of about 35°. These cliffs are highest in the south and west, where they reach above 1,100 feet. To the north the height decreases, and the northernmost extensions of the plateau merge into the general plains. Long branching wadis have cut deep into the heart of the plateau, and in one or two places have cut right across it. In some places, particularly to the west, the desert plains extend unbroken up to the base of the cliffs, but at others the plateau is screened behind a maze of detached fragments and dissected hills. (Peel 1941, 8).

To Peel, the outstanding feature of the Gilf was the abrupt distinction between desert floor and plateau surface: the two levels seemed to be entirely distinct, with no transition between them.

Access to the top was rendered difficult by the steep boundary cliffs, but the effort was worthwhile:

Upon the top the Gilf forces on one the complete illusion of a large cliff-girt island rising from mid-ocean: the endless succession of headlands all of even height, the cliff beneath them falling sheer from the flatness of the tableland without preliminary drainage slope, the limitless plains 1,000 feet below, so far down that their negligible yellow features fade away in the haze. Even more striking is the monotonous shouting of the wind that sweeps continually over the plateau and swirls away into space over the edge of the cliffs: nothing could better imitate the roar of breakers on a distant beach. Another odd fancy was the imagined presence of the old people. There was nothing between them and us. The place has the utter remoteness of another world. One felt suspended high above the desert below, itself many hundreds of miles from the nearest habitation. The plateau is a harsh barrenness of broken rock; over all its thousands of square miles we found but two or there tiny dells containing vegetation, yet a network of paths cross and recross it. (Bagnold 1939, 284).

The abrupt rise of the Gilf Kebir is made all the more remarkable because of the fact that it arises above a desert surface that is immensely flat – the so-called Selima Sand Sheet. This covers about 120,000 km² and is a largely featureless surface of lag-gravels and fine sand broken only by widely separated dune fields and giant ripples. It was thus described by Peel:

> Covering an area of at least 3,000 square miles, this region appears to the eye absolutely flat and featureless save for an occasional line of sand dunes. In reality it slopes very gently eastwards towards the Nile, but for scores of miles no feature larger than a tiny pebble breaks the uniformity of the surface. The solid rock is everywhere covered with a uniform sheet of wind-blown sand, which is probably nowhere more than a few feet thick: the sandstone beneath it would appear to have been worn down almost to a true plain. (Peel 1941, 6).

Some indication of the nature of this astonishing country may be given by the fact that while crossing it on one occasion Peel and his colleagues drove their Ford V-8 cars at a consistent speed of 60 to 70 kph for three hours on end without once having to slacken speed or deviate from their compass course.

In 1935 Bill Shaw had also crossed the Selima Sand Sheet and recounted:

> It is impossible to convey any idea of the absolute desolation of this vast plain of hard yellow sand over which one can drive for scores of miles in any direction as fast as a car will go. Lack of contrast and natural features make photography useless…one could look as far as the horizon in all directions seeing nothing but a waste of level sand, no dunes, no hills, no valleys, not a stone the size of an egg to break the monotony of desolation. (Anon 1935, 462).

Bagnold reported that on one occasion, such was the tedium of "this utterly flat sheet of firm sand" that driving at speed hour after hour, on a compass bearing, it became hard to stay awake. On one occasion both drivers of a car fell asleep, the driver's foot remaining hard down on the pedal. They were only retrieved after an anxious chase (Bagnold 1990, 66).

The origin of the sand sheet is a subject that is far from tedious, however, but everyone agrees that it is the product of a very long history of erosion and aggradation (accumulation of sediment) by river and wind processes (see, for example, Maxwell and Haynes 2001).

Ronald Peel (1912-1985), who accompanied Bagnold on the 1938 expedition as a surveyor, was a graduate of St Catharine's College, Cambridge, where he distinguished himself with a first class degree in Geography and Anthropology. He also showed sufficient prowess in cricket and rugby to earn membership of the elite Hawks' Club. He was an elegant, pipe-smoking, charming, scholarly but diffident individual, invariably well dressed but never happier than when lying under a car engine in his overalls. His experiences with Bagnold, which included stripping a gearbox down in a sandstorm, moulded his subsequent academic career, and he became Britain's leading desert geomorphologist in the immediate post-war years. He went on to hold chairs in Geography at Leeds and Bristol (Haggett 1986). His contributions to the 1938 expedition included surveying and some archaeological and anthropological studies, including a discussion of the Tibu peoples who had previously roamed the area. He also developed some novel ideas on the role of surface runoff and groundwater sapping in producing the remarkable landscape of the Gilf Kebir.

One feature of the Bagnold expeditions is that besides exploring new regions and developing new techniques for desert travel he also had time for science. Not only did he use the 1938 expedition to validate his own wind tunnel experiments. He also brought with him people who had expertise in geomorphology, archaeology, anthropology and geology. The participation of the archaeologist Oliver H. Myers on the 1938 expedition was sponsored by the chemist and Egyptologist, Sir Robert Mond. Myers found lithic and ceramic materials that were not fully analysed until the 1970s. Hans Winkler made a survey of rock art, which was something that interested Peel as well.

Some expeditions can be self-indulgent stunts in which alpha males display their virility. Not so with Bagnold. His team made remarkable discoveries that included the profusion of archaeological sites and the evidence of profound changes in past climatic conditions. Both Bagnold and Peel made fundamental contributions to desert geomorphology.

Indeed, Bagnold wrote the classic book on dunes in 1941 and it is still much cited today. He attributed his fascination for dunes directly to the experience of motoring into the interior of an exceptionally dry desert. The development of motor transport made it possible to study in the further interiors of the great deserts the free interplay of wind and sand, uncomplicated by the effects of moisture, vegetation, or of fauna, and to observe the results of that interplay extended over great periods of time:

> Here, instead of finding chaos and disorder, the observer never fails to be amazed by a simplicity of form, and exactitude of repetition and a geometric order unknown in nature on a scale larger than that of crystalline structure. In places vast accumulations of sand weighing millions of tons move inexorably, in regular formation, over the surface of the country, growing, retaining their shape, even breeding, in a manner which, by its grotesque imitation of life, is vaguely disturbing to an imaginative mind. Elsewhere the dunes are cut to another pattern – lined up in parallel ranges, peak following peak in regular succession like the teeth of a monstrous saw for scores, even hundreds of miles, without a break and without a change in direction, over a landscape so flat that their formation cannot be influenced by any local geographical features. Or again we find smaller forms, rare among the coastal sand hills, consisting of rows of coarse-grained ridges even more regular than dunes. Over large areas of accumulated sand the loose, dry, uncemented grains are so firmly packed that a loaded lorry driven across the surface makes tracks less than an inch in depth. Then, without the slightest visual indication of change, the substance only a few inches

ahead is found to be dry quicksand through which no vehicle can force its way. (Bagnold 1941, xxi).

Bagnold also experienced some of the very strange sounds that dunes can make. Many other travellers have also heard similar 'singing sands': He reported that at times, especially on a still evening after a windy day, the dunes would emit, suddenly, spontaneously, and for many minutes, a low-pitched sound so penetrating that normal speech could be heard only with difficulty.

The W.B. Kennedy Shaw
Expedition of 1935

Not all the expeditions of the 1930s involved Bagnold, for some of his colleagues made their own forays into the desert using cars adapted to the Bagnold model. Notable was the Kennedy Shaw expedition of 1935, Besides Bill Shaw, it included Rupert Harding-Newman, Ronnie McEuen, and Michael Mason (figure 42), and Colonel and Mrs George Strutt. They were a varied lot. Bill Shaw (1901-1979) had entered the Sudan Civil service in 1924 as a forestry official, but then became a professional archaeologist. He was described by Michael Mason as "slight and well made; neither tall nor short; long-legged for his height, active and very enduring; gentle in speech and by nature silent". Rupert Harding-Newman of the Royal Tank Corps, on the other hand, was described as small, but with a tremendously enduring and powerful frame, and as "gay, adequate, reliable and imperturbable" and tempering "a reckless fearlessness by an unusual degree of common sense". Ronnie McEuen was tall and thin, fair-haired, talkative and cheerful, stammered, had one lung, and was an archaeologist by profession. Michael Mason, who had an injured leg, was a gifted author, with a knowledge of animals. George Strutt was older, but an inveterate big-game hunter, fisherman and lover of wild life. His young wife, Mary, "gentlest of women, was hard as nails when it came to physical endurance." (Mason 1936, 19).

This was a very lengthy expedition (map 11) that took in the Gilf Kebir, Uweinat and the Wadi Howar (the last in the northern Sudan) but returned to Cairo via the Great Sand Sea and the Siwa oasis. In all they travelled 10,000 km of which half had been through unexplored country. The Wadi Howar, a wide ribbon of vegetation cutting through the desert, was found to be teeming with game, with undersized lion and packs of wild dogs. Shaw tells how they shot three of these dogs and afterwards left baits of meat poisoned with strychnine (*The Times*, 7 August 1935).

Figure 42. Bill, Rupert, Ronnie and Mike.

Sometimes the going was very tough, and Shaw recounted just how difficult it was to cross the dunes that barred the entrance to the Wadi Hamra on the eastern side of the Gilf Kebir. Six miles (9.6 km) were accomplished in as many hours:

> They were the worst dunes I had ever crossed. The whole day we had been forcing a way through soft sand, using 5ft. steel channels and rope ladders laid out to form a track for the wheels, at times completely unloading a car and making a porterage round a bad place, or slowly feeling our way on foot, marking with small heaps of sand a route between the 'liquid' patches. (*The Times*, 6 August 1935).

Shaw was intrigued by the wadis:

> Although from the west the Gilf presents a line of continuous cliffs, on the east it is cut up by broad sandy valleys. It is asthough an army of gigantic maggots, advancing from the east, had eaten their way into the plateau as into a flat cheese…(ibid.).

137

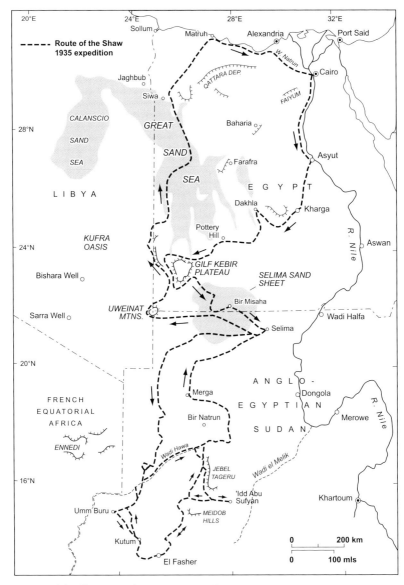

Map 11. The Shaw Expedition route, 1935.

Figure 43. One of the Shaw Expedition Model A Fords transits a dune.

The tussocky sub-desert belt south of 17 degrees was another troubling type of terrain

> Hard-based tussocks of long grass and small dry rain runnels force one to bump over them for hours in low or second gear....once I counted Harding-Newman change gear 190 times in 10 miles. Cars are not built to stand this sort of thing for long. (*The Times*, 7 August 1935).

In spite of such terrain, their three Fords performed well (figure 43), carrying loads over 10,000 kg and achieving a petrol consumption that was a shade over 4.6 km per litre. The nine inch wide Dunlop 'airwheels' proved to be especially effective in the Great Sand Sea. Shaw was generally very struck by how durable the cars were:

> There are only two ways in which a car might become a total loss in the Libyan Desert – by fire or by getting into a hollow in the dunes with sides too steep and soft to surmount. Then the only solution would be to take the car to pieces and carry it out. Fortunately the regular arrangement of the dune-ranges does not favour the formation of such a trap. (*The Times*, 8 August 1935).

The expedition made some useful archaeological and zoological discoveries. Unfortunately, it was also marred by tragedy, as Shaw reported (1936, 198). It was near the north side of the Wadi Hawa that Strutt met with an accident. In a fall from the running-board of a slowly moving car he broke two ribs which pierced his lung. They were then nearly 500 km from El Fasher, the nearest point at which they could hope to find medical aid. They started for El Fasher on the second morning after the accident, and on the evening of the following day were in Kutum, the head-quarters of the Northern Darfur District. McEuen and Shaw went on to El Fasher that night, and on the following morning Captain G.L. Prendergast, a member of many Bagnold expeditions and now attached to the Western Arab Corps, flew out to Kutum in his private aeroplane and brought Strutt back. A dust-storm was blowing and the flight was a fine piece of work in conditions of very low visibility. Strutt remained in hospital in El Fasher for three weeks. At first his condition improved, but later complications arose, and on 6 March he was moved by RAF plane to Khartoum where he died on 25 March.

Michael Mason was moved by Strutt's death, describing the colonel (1936, 216) as:

> …the type of English country gentleman who is loved by his tenants, adored by his servants, never left alone by his neighbours and respected by everybody. He was the kind of sportsman who searches till darkness rather than leave a wounded partridge, and lies out in the snow sooner that leave a wounded stag. (*The Times*, 6 August 1935).

It was curious how English gentlemen of that generation could be so good to animals but hunt them and shoot them at every opportunity.

Bill Shaw wrote up the expedition for *The Times* (6, 7, 8 August 1935). He stressed the importance of tinned food:

In the Libyan Desert there can be no living off the country; in the south one may get an occasional gazelle or a clutch of new-laid ostrich eggs, but for the rest all food has to come out of a tin. Fortunately the quality and variety obtainable today are excellent, and a diet of tinned food, supported by Kharga dates and the unjustly despised Army biscuit, leaves nothing to complain of.

Almásy and the Claytons

Not all the explorers were English gentlemen. Count László Ede Almásy, 'Teddy' to his friends, was one of the most intriguing of the desert motorists, and was the figure upon which the fictional novel and film by Michael Ondaatje, *The English Patient* (1992), were based. His extraordinary life has been pieced together by John Bierman in *The Secret Life of László Almásy* (2004). Born of an Austro-Hungarian aristocratic family in Borostyanko (Bernstein in Eastern Austria) in 1895, he was a big-boned, blue eyed, chain-smoking, hawk-nosed man who walked with drooping shoulders and had a nervous tic. He developed an interest in motorised transport while at a 'crammer', a rather undistinguished private boarding school in Eastbourne, southern England, where he gained his first pilot's licence at the age of seventeen and formed close ties with the Boy Scout movement. He served in the Austro-Hungarian forces in the First World War and became a much-decorated pilot. After the war he claimed that he had been made a Count by the exiled Karl IV, the last of the Hapsburg kings. After the War he also worked among other things for the Steyr Company and in 1926, to demonstrate the capabilities of their vehicles, he drove a car in the company of Prince Antal Eszterházy along the Nile and into the Sudan.

In 1929 with Prince Ferdinand Von Lichtenstein, the English industrialist Anthony Brunner, and the Austrian newsreel cameraman Rudi Mayer, he drove down from Wadi Halfa to Selima Oasis along the Darb el Arba'in and in 1930 conducted motor car trials for the Sudan Government between Wadi Halfa and Uweinat. He also visited Kufra, where the Italians believed he was a British spy. Other expeditions in 1935 took him along the Darb el Arba'in to Wadi Howar and across the Great Sand Sea from Ain Dalla to Siwa. On that journey, one of his colleagues was a German, Hansjoachim von der Esch, an alumnus of Christ Church, Oxford, and one of the first Germans to study at Oxford University after the first world war.

Figure 44. Sir Robert Clayton-East-Clayton.

Von der Esch wrote up this and other explorations in *Weenak – die Karavane ruft* (1944). He was no mean photographer, and he provided many of the plates in Almásy's book on his great journeys *Unbekannte Sahara* (1939). The 1935 journey was effectively the last that Almásy undertook before his exploits in the Second World War, and the British authorities, possibly sensing that he might be involved in espionage activities, seemed unwilling to give him the necessary travel permits. However, he remained in Egypt, setting up a glider and aviation school in Cairo. In 1937 he flew the first glider over the Pyramids.

Almásy was a great hunter, as well as being an explorer, aviator, and motor enthusiast. In 1932 he joined up with Sir Robert Clayton-East-Clayton (figure 44) (the Geoffrey Clifton of *The English Patient*), a naval man, owner of an aircraft (a second hand Gypsy Moth called *Rupert*) and, in spite of just having married a young wife, looking for adventure. They decided on an expedition to find the legendary lost oasis of Zerzura. They combined the use of cars and Clayton-East-Clayton's aircraft, to make a reconnaissance of the Gilf Kebir plateau in southern Egypt. It was arranged that Major Pat Clayton (no relation) would help them and they were also joined by Wing-Commander Penderel. Shortly after the expedition, which explored the western side of the Gilf Kebir, Sir Robert died suddenly and prematurely, on 2 September 1932. He had only got married on 29 February of that year.

Sir Robert's beautiful young widow, Dorothy, a vicar's daughter, flew out to Egypt in 1933 to continue her late husband's work. She bought two Fords and joined Major Clayton on a journey to Kufra, Siwa and the Great Sand Sea. At Kufra she was struck by the hospitality offered by the Italian Air Force, but she noted that some of the villages of Kufra seemed to be depleted of the Arab population, "the uncompromising fanaticism of the Sennusiya making it difficult for them to live at close quarters with the Italians". She was also impressed by the way her Fords coped with the Gilf Kebir:

> We returned from Kufra to the Gilf and made a survey of the top of the plateau. The car was successfully got up the steep cliffs, but getting it down again nearly ended in tragedy. With all the brakes jammed on and the whole crew holding on for all they were worth the feat of tobogganing it down was accomplished. This finally convinced us that there is no country which cannot be traversed with a little optimism and a Ford lorry. (Dorothy Clayton-East-Clayton, posthumous article in *The Times*, 16 September 1933, 11).

Tragedy struck her as well on her return to England. She was killed in a flying accident on 15 September 1933 at Brooklands, the racecourse near Weybridge in Surrey, England, which was also one of Britain's first airfields. The accident was a curious one, for as her aircraft was taxiing along the runway at around 80 kph, she leapt out of it. At the inquest a verdict of death by misadventure was returned.

The British authorities were sometimes suspicious about Almásy's activities in the 1930s and about the company he kept. For example, a document records the doubts that the Cairo Chancery expressed to the Egyptian Department of the Foreign Office concerning the nature of von der Esch's involvement:

Herr von der Esch is a rather mysterious man. He is a German from Wurtemberg about 36 years old. He served in the German army during the War and was one of the first Germans to go to Oxford again after the war. He was at the 'House' [Christ Church, Oxford] and while there met his future wife, an attractive Swede, who was learning English in North Oxford at the time. His father is still alive and lives in Wurtemberg, but Herr von der Esch does not often go back to Germany. In conversation he and his wife profess little sympathy for the Nazis and they have been in fact 'mal vu' by the local German colony on this account. Nevertheless they go about a great deal with the German Minister and Frau von Stohrer and are in very close contact with the Legation. They see a great deal of the English residents here both Army and civilian and get on very well with them. Nevertheless no one seems to know quite what von der Esch is doing here and why he chooses to live in Cairo. He is ostensibly employed in the local branch of the 'Maschinen Fabrick Augsburg-Nuremburg' but the Commercial Secretariat have never been able to trace any salesmanship on his part. The firm have a competent Manager and Assistant Manager and von der Esch's connection with it is rather hard to fathom. On the other hand nothing definitely sinister has been discovered about von der Esch. He spends a good deal of his spare time, of which he seems to have a lot, in making motor expeditions to the desert and this fact may explain his participation in the Almásy expedition. (Public Record Office Ref. FO371/18034).

Bill Kennedy Shaw, intelligence officer of the LRDG, summarised his views on whether Almásy was a spy as follows:

I think all the governments interested in the Libyan Desert – British, Egyptian, Italian – wondered if Almásy was a spy working for the other side. The Italian officials in Kufra were careless and when the French captured the oasis they found in the archives, foolishly unburnt, enough evidence to put Almásy into a concentration camp if not up against a wall. But even so I doubt if he really was an agent in the Italians' pay and in any case they did not trust him for on his return to Cairo after his expedition in 1933 they managed, by an ingenious trick which the Kufra papers describe, to steal a copy of his maps and his report. (Shaw 1945, 169).

Whether a spy or not, his MI5 file was not very flattering, describing Almásy as "very ugly and shabbily dressed, with a fat and pendulous nose, drooping shoulders and a nervous tic".

One of the greatest explorers of the Western Desert was Patrick Andrew Clayton (1896-1962). He first went to Egypt in 1915 with the Army Service Corps and returned there in 1920 as a topographer with the Geological Department of the Survey of Egypt. In 1923 he joined the Desert Surveys Department under Dr Ball, and started to use Fords in his work. One of these was a Ford Model TT (long wheel-base truck) called *Fanny*. In the next few years he was concerned with the demarcation of the border between Egypt and Libya. From 1927 to 1930 he was involved with mapping the Qattara Depression, which had been discovered as extending below sea level by fellow surveyor George Walpole in 1924. In 1930/31, equipped with the new Model A Ford he was down at Uweinat and the Gilf Kebir. On 29 August 1931, while on leave in London, he attended the first 'Zerzura Dinner' at the Café Royal in London. Among those present, apart from Clayton, were R. Bagnold, J. Ball, V.F. Craig, R.G.L. Giblin, V.C. Holland, W.J. Harding King, D. Newbold and G. Prendergast. Ten years later many of them would be with the LRDG.

In 1932 Clayton accompanied the 'Zerzura 1' Expedition organised by Almásy and Sir Robert Clayton-East-Clayton. The following season he made his first attempt to master the Great Sand Sea. He went westwards from Ain Dalla, further than Bagnold had in 1930, and emerged on the far side of the Sand Sea. Here 'Big Cairn' was erected. Their new route was to become important when the LRDG entered Italian territory during the Second World War.

In 1933 he accompanied Lady Dorothy Clayton-East-Clayton to Ain Dalla, Kufra and Siwa. In the same year Almásy went to the

Gilf Kebir with Wing Commander Penderel (see Penderel, 1934) and various others, including Richard Bermann. Bermann was an Austrian author and journalist, who also used the pseudonym, Arnold Höllriegel. He was a great hater of the Nazi regime and eventually fled to the USA. With Almásy and Count Ludovico di Caporiacco he made great discoveries of cave paintings (Bermann 1934). It seems that it was just as well that there were two separate expeditions for Lady Clayton had developed an aversion to Almásy and had detected his supposed homosexual tendencies (Clayton 1998, 63).

Later in the 1930s, as Egyptianization of Government departments progressed, Clayton decided it was time to move on and from 1938 to 1940 he served in Tanganyika Territory as a Surveyor. In 1940 fellow surveyor George Walpole offered him a job in Trans-Jordan, but before he could take it up he was summoned to Cairo. In July, with the rank of Captain, he joined the fledgling LRDG. After heroic work, for which Wavell awarded him the DSO, Clayton was captured by the Italians near Kufra and was imprisoned in mainland Italy. One of his visitors there was Count Almásy. As Corbyn wrote:

> …south of Kufra, his small column of five or six cars was observed by a scouting Italian aeroplane, and was attacked by a column of armoured cars from Kufra, losing three vehicles. The remainder, circling northward in at attempt to withdraw, were bombed from the air. The gallant Clayton's car was hit and he himself severely wounded, and made prisoner with most of his men. (Corbyn 1944, 21).

Four of his men, however, evaded capture and with only 10 pints (5.6 litres) of water between them set off on foot on the 400 km journey to French territory. After 11 days they were rescued by the French. Corbyn relates that "One of these gallant men died four days later, and one lost his reason; the other two only asked to be sent back at once to the front".

Peniakoff

Vladimir Peniakoff (1897-1951), a year younger than Bagnold, was one of the only exponents of solo travel in the desert. He was born in Belgium to Russian émigré parents, but in 1914 went up to St John's College, Cambridge. However, he left at the end of his fourth term so that he could enlist in the French army, where he developed a clear distaste for the French. He accused them (Peniakoff 1950, 29) of "meanness, pretentious vulgarity, devastating selfishness, parochialism, bogus culture, surliness and conceit". If ever he had to fight again, he had decided it would most certainly not be for the French. He was invalided out of their army shortly after the 1918 armistice and then trained as an engineer. In 1924 he settled in Egypt and devoted many years to the manufacture of sugar. A man of powerful views and a raging temper, he hated the dreary life of local Europeans, Levantines and westernised Egyptians:

> Endeavour is limited to fierce, unimaginative money-making and the more unrewarding forms of vanity. The thrills of love are provided by a season ticket at the brothel and mechanical affairs with the dry, metallic, coldly lecherous wives of your friends. No hobbies. Games are played, to be sure, out of snobbishness, copying the English. Adventure is provided by daily sessions of bridge, rummy or poker, and gambling on the Cotton Exchange. (Ibid.).

On the other hand, he admired the simple country folk – the *fellahin* and the *badawin*.

From 1925-28 he worked at a sugar mill north of Luxor. This gave him a great deal of leisure and he read Palgrave, Burton, Doughty, Lawrence, Gertrude Bell and other great writers on the exploration of Arabia. In 1930 he transferred to the Hawamdiah sugar refinery outside Cairo. It was then that he learnt about the journeys that Bagnold and his friends were making and saw that he too could be an explorer.

Peniakoff owned a two-seater Model A Ford sedan which he converted into a box-body truck with balloon tyres. He called it the *Pisspot* and travelled over 190,000 km in it before it came to a sticky end at Mersa Matruh in the second year of the Second World War.

Going against the rules of Bagnold and his teams, he travelled in just one car and generally alone. He built a sun-compass, obtained a theodolite, a stop-watch, a small dry-cell commercial wireless set and a nautical almanac. With these he taught himself dead-reckoning navigation. Going alone he had to be meticulous in his preparations:

> I had made up my mind that on no account would I rely on search parties to rescue me if I got lost or ran out of petrol or break down. To make quite certain that such a disgrace wouldn't happen to me I never let anybody know to what area of the desert I intended going. I carried an impressive number of spare parts for the truck and I made sure, at home, that I could fix them single-handed. I endeavoured to provide for the most unlikely accidents, and as a result I overloaded my poor Pisspot to such an extent that I nearly broke its back. Practically the only spare I didn't carry was a cylinder block. (Ibid., 26).

He also invented a pram in the hope that this might help him escape in the event of an emergency with the *Pisspot*. He explained that more through persistent good luck than skill, he had so far always succeeded in bringing his truck home, but he knew that he could not eliminate completely the possibility of a breakdown or of getting hopelessly bogged. As the range of his trips increased and took him 250 km or more into the desert, he got worried about the means of walking back in case he had to abandon his truck. He had no doubts about his ability to find his way back to the Nile Valley, for him one of the simplest of problems, but he had to drink and eat on the way out and he did not fancy a 20 kg rucksack. A young schoolmaster friend called Jeffrey Bunn found the answer for him. His fancy had been to walk in the desert, and for his water, kit and food, he had built himself a hand-cart mounted on motor-cycle wheels which he had once pushed all the way from Ma'adi, near Cairo, to Sokhna, on the Red Sea coast, taking a week over the trip and living in comfort. Peniakoff had a similar 'pram' made of aluminium tubing; it could be dismantled and stored in the back of his truck, and with a sufficient reserve of water and food he felt justified in taking his lonely trips further into the Western Desert than he had ever done before.

In 1939 he planned to go to Uweinat, but with war looming and a desire to fight for the British this time, he decided instead to try and join up. However, his lone peace-time driving exploits were to prove of inestimable value in the years to come.

The Long Range Desert Group

Archibald Wavell (1883-1950), who recruited both Orde Wingate and Ralph Bagnold to undertake special operations during the Second World War, was an army officer who had served both in the Boer and First World Wars, during which he had lost an eye. "He was not a man of social graces and his silences and inability to hide his boredom were proverbial" (Dear and Foot 2001, 991). Moreover, a mutual antipathy rose between him and Prime Minister Winston Churchill, but notwithstanding this, he had a hugely distinguished career in which he was Commander in Chief of the Middle East during the early part of the campaign in the Western Desert and subsequently became Viceroy of India, an Earl and a Field Marshal. Wavell, like Bagnold, was not only a soldier, but also a scholar and an original thinker. Wavell was even a connoisseur and writer of poetry. He was not an orthodox soldier. He said that his ideal infantryman was a cross between a poacher, a gunman and a cat-burglar.

The story of how Wavell and Bagnold came together to set up the LRDG (figure 45) is an intriguing one. When war broke out in September 1939, Major Bagnold was recalled to the Army. Notwithstanding his obvious potential utility in the Middle East or North Africa, the army dispatched him to Kenya, a country of which he knew virtually nothing. However, a higher power recognised better than the Army where his talents should be employed. The troop ship taking him to Kenya, the great and luxurious Cunarder, *Franconia*, as it worked its way across the Mediterranean was involved in a serious collision with the *Alcantara*. It was so badly damaged that it had to disembark its cargo of passengers at an Egyptian port, where they were required to wait for a passage on another ship. Bagnold seized his chance, took the train to Cairo and met up with old chums in the social mecca of army officers, Shepheard's Hotel. Here he was spotted by a reporter from the *Egyptian Gazette*, who reported his presence and recounted some of his past exploits in Egypt.

Figure 45. The logo of the Long Range Desert Group.

Figure 46. Orlando Lorenzini.

152

General Wavell read this piece and so was alerted to Bagnold's presence in the capital.

Wavell's own presence in Cairo at that time had no official status, but he was working behind the scenes developing schemes for the expansion of the war in the region. He was also planning to see what could be done if Italy, which occupied neighbouring Libya, should enter the war. He himself occupied a small office in the attic of the headquarters building of British Troops Egypt (BTE). It was to this office that the glass-eyed Wavell summoned the Major:

The interview was brief but decisive.

"Good morning Bagnold. I know about you. Been posted to Kenya. Know anything about that country?"

"No sir."

"Be more useful here wouldn't you?"

"Yes sir"

"Right. That's all for now." (Constable 1999, 4).

Two days later Bagnold was transferred to the Egyptian theatre rather than the Kenyan one. He was posted to Mersa Matruh on the Egyptian Mediterranean coast. It was at Mersa Matruh that C.S. Jarvis had seen service in the Light Car Patrols in the previous war.

Bagnold appreciated two things. One was the profound weakness of the British defences. The other was the alarming threat that was posed to Egypt and the Sudan by the presence of the huge Italian forces in Libya and Ethiopia. Could the Italians make a thrust to the Suez Canal and the Nile Delta in the north? Could they mount a raid from their garrison at Uweinat eastwards to the Nile, seizing the Aswan Dam, holding Egypt to ransom and isolating it from Sudan? Bagnold also knew that the Italian soldier, Colonel Lorenzini (figure 46), whom he had met at Sarra in the Western Desert eight years previously, and whom he appreciated as being clever and daring, would have similar thoughts that would be expressed to the Italian High Command in Libya. Lorenzini himself fought bravely in the war, but was finally killed in battle by the British at the Heights of Keren in Ethiopia in March 1941. His head was blown off. He was buried at the place of his death and colleagues placed his boots, spurs and sword on his grave.

The Italians had developed their own capability of motoring in the desert, with their Auto-Saharan company employing Fiat armoured cars and light vehicles for reconnaissance. Moreover, Bagnold realised how difficult it would be to monitor Italian movements in the Uweinat area given that the British then had no aircraft with sufficient range to undertake reconnaissance.

Bagnold's appreciation of the Italian threat was shared by his companion and historian of the LRDG, Bill Kennedy Shaw. Shaw was especially concerned about the strategic significance of Kufra Oasis in eastern Libya, which, 1,100 km west of the Nile was secure from attack behind the twin barriers of the Sand Sea and Gilf Kebir Plateau, with plentiful water and good communications to the coast. There the enemy could build up a considerable force. Beyond Kufra was Uweinat with its good though limited water and its landing grounds. From Uweinat to Wadi Halfa was three days' run over excellent going. In the summer of 1940 a force of one or two hundred determined men could have attacked and taken Wadi Halfa, wrecked the dockyard and the railway workshops, sunk any river steamers or barges and made a mess of the Egypt-Sudan line of communications at that point.

In addition to the threat to the Nile, there was also the threat to West Africa:

From Kufra too, is the line of approach to the Chad Province of French Equatorial Africa from Sarra and Faya. And through the Chad Province ran the West African-Middle East air route, the chain of airfields between Takoradi and Cairo along which so many hundreds of aircraft were flown when the Mediterranean was closed. An Italian force moving down from Kufra and, farther west, from Murzuk in June, 1940, winning over the hesitant French and capturing Fort Lamy, would have been very hard to dislodge at a time when we needed every man and truck for the defence of Egypt and the Sudan. (Shaw 2000, 13-14).

Bagnold prepared a position paper on how to counteract this grave strategic threat, but initially it was either ignored, rejected or ridiculed by the hidebound, tarmac warriors in Cairo. His proposal to establish car patrols to cross the tarmac-free wastes of the Western Desert got nowhere.

The resentment that emerged about the obstructive tactics and lack of vision amongst certain Cairo officers emerged in a wartime poem. In it there are two, presumably fictional, brothers, Aubrey and St John Poop. The former joined the LRDG and made the ultimate sacrifice:

Meanwhile his brother, St John Poop,
Had joined the *Short* Range Desert Group
Which keeps the Pyramids in sight
From Mena House on Sunday night
And based on Shepheards, moves no nearer
Wide open spaces than Gezirah.
Here St John proved a great success
And ran a really slap-up mess,
Which may explain, for all I know,
His Colonelcy and DSO. (Page 1976, 174-5).

However, in June 1940, France collapsed and Italy declared war. Marshal Rodolfo Graziani (figure 47), the dedicated Fascist butcher of Sanussi and Ethiopian alike, had just succeeded Marshal Italo Balbo, who had been accidentally shot down and killed by his own anti-aircraft battery over Tobruk. Graziani's 15 divisions were poised to strike, the Mediterranean and the Gulf of Suez were virtually closed down to shipping, and Egypt was effectively isolated. Wavell, whose available froces were outnumbered by about ten to

Figure 47. Graziani – he was not as nice as he looked.

one, was however now out of his attic and was Commander in Chief of the Middle East. On 19 June 1940 Bagnold dug out the last dog-eared copy of his proposal for car patrols, persuaded the head of the Operation Staff to place it personally on Wavell's table, and waited. He did not have to wait for long. Within an hour he was again alone with the Commander-in-Chief. This time the meeting lasted longer but, it was no less decisive. Bagnold recounted what happened:

> Wavell was alone. He waved me to an armchair and, picking up my memo, said quietly, "Tell me more about this." Knowing Wavell had served on Allenby's staff in Egypt during the last war, I mentioned the present lack of anything corresponding to the Light Car Patrols that would be able to give warning of possible attacks from the then unknown west. I told him

briefly of the great range of action possible by small self-contained parties that had been especially trained and equipped. Such parties could operate anywhere in the uninhabited interior of Libya and Egypt and could read tracks to find out if any offensive action against southern Egypt was in preparation. (Bagnold 1990, 124).

At first Wavell seemed a bit sceptical and asked, "What would you do if you found no such preparations?" Bagnold said, "How about some piracy in the high desert?" At the word 'piracy,' Wavell's rather grim face suddenly broke into a broad grin. Without a moment of reflection he said, "Can you be ready in six weeks?" Taken aback, Bagnold said, "Yes Sir, provided…" He said, "Yes, of course. There'll be opposition and delay?" He pressed his bell. Sir Arthur Smith, his chief of staff came in. "Arthur, Bagnold seeks a talisman. Get this typed out now, for my signature." He dictated, "To all heads of departments and branches. I wish any request by Major Bagnold in person to be granted immediately and without question." Then, turning to Bagnold he said, "When you are ready, write out your operation orders and bring them to me personally. I'll countersign them. Remember, not a word of this must get out. We are in a foreign country and there are sixty thousand enemy subjects going about freely. I can't stop them. Go to my DMI [Director of Military Intelligence] and get a good cover story."

Bagnold left the meeting somewhat astounded at the *carte blanche* he had been offered. There had been only two queries:

How was I proposing to get into Libya? I told him, "Straight through the middle of the sand sea. It's safe because it's believed to be impassable." His other query had concerned the climate. Could white troops survive the summer temperatures and sand storms? I told him that was indeed a bit of a gamble, but the right sort of men could stand anything. (Ibid., 125).

He pondered why the great man had given his midget proposal such priority, but then remembered that Wavell was the leading exponent of strategic deception. Faced with the probability of being attacked in overwhelming numbers by the Italians, he was going to delay the enemy by bluff until he could get reinforcements from India and South Africa, if not from England. He would exploit the one great Italian weakness: the immense, undefended length of their single coastal supply road. At the same time, this would reawaken their old fear of attack from the unknown interior that had for some years confined them to enclaves along the coastal strip. The small unit Bagnold proposed, with its remarkable mobility and endurance, could create a threat out of proportion to reality, even though that mobility would greatly limit firepower. They would be able to carry nothing heavier than machine guns and some land mines, both useless against walled forts. However, it would be enough if Bagnold's people were to create the impression of British ubiquity throughout the interior of Libya.

Having only six weeks at his disposal, Bagnold had to work fast, and work fast he did. On 5 August, the Long Range Patrols, as they were initially named, left Cairo on their first training trip. On 27 August they were ready for action. To enable this to happen, one of his first acts was to seek the help of his pre-war travelling companions. Fortunately one of them, Rupert Harding-Newman was actually in Cairo, serving as a liaison officer with the Egyptian Army. Unfortunately he was not released. Bill Kennedy Shaw was relatively close at hand as he was Curator of the Jerusalem Museum. Pat Clayton was surveying in Tanganyika. He too was located, summoned and then flown to Cairo. Shaw and Clayton, both of whom knew how to conquer the Great Sand Sea, were both in Cairo within three days of Bagnold's call and were immediately commissioned as army captains. Guy Prendergast was not available – he was in London – but he joined them six months later.

The ability to navigate in the often featureless and badly mapped desert was a major priority, and Shaw's prime task was to train navigators from scratch in dead-reckoning, astronomical position finding, and route mapping. The lack of useful maps was a particular problem in Libya. Bill Shaw (2000, 24-25) believed that the Italian maps of Libya reflected the Italian national character in its aspects of bombast and self-assurance. He recounted that there here was no nonsense about the petty details of topography on these sheets. Many of them were obviously based on air observations (but not on an air survey), and after a few flights across the country a cartographer had roughed in a range of mountains here and a sand sea or two there. The mountains that were drawn in were all high "as became the dignity of Fascist Italy". Shaw expressed a certain grudging admiration for Captain Marchesi of the Istituto Geografico Militare, the equivalent of our Ordinance Survey, who made the 1:100,000 map of Jalo:

> Marchesi, I am sure, was a realist. Jalo, he felt, was a one-eyed hole of which no map was really needed. The sand was soft and the day hot, so why worry? Marchesi put his feet up on the mess table, shouted for another drink, and drew his map. It is just possible that the absurd inaccuracies were a deep plot to mislead out attacking forces, but it seems hardly likely that the Italians had thought of that as long ago as 1931. (Shaw 2000, 24-25).

So, the crucial thing was not so much map-reading, something to which the army mind was generally well attuned, but navigation, itself more normally a naval or airforce skill. Thus Bagnold's team had to obtain a series of unorthodox stores. As the patrols would need to navigate by the stars over trackless desert, Air Almanacs were requisitioned. Theodolites had to be obtained to enable accurate position-fixing by the stars at the end of each day's journey. This was far from easy. The British Army in the Middle East provided just one, George Murray of the Desert Surveys produced another, and a third had to be flown in from Nairobi. Sun compasses were also required. Luckily the Egyptian Army had procured a store of the model developed by Bagnold for his inter-war journeys and he was able to borrow some of his own invention from them.

Finding appropriate vehicles was a still more fundamental and frustrating task. To enable sufficient supplies to be carried and to permit

Figure 48. 30 cwt Chevrolet of the LRDG preserved in the Imperial War Museum.

the transport of guns, mines, ammunition, radios and all the paraphernalia of war, something larger than the pre-war Model T and Model A Fords was required. The Chevrolet Motor Company had been competing madly with Ford since it was established in 1911 and by 1927, on a global basis, it was outselling Ford, as it was for the next half century. It provided the answer. After trying out several types and makes of vehicle, Bagnold settled on 30 cwt Chevrolet trucks with two-wheel drive (figure 48). Existing four-wheel drive vehicles were rejected as being too heavy and having too great a thirst for fuel. As a result their range was inadequate. The Jeep, which was to be much used by the SAS and LRDG in later years, was not yet in production. In any case, the pre-war journeys had shown what two-wheel drive vehicles could achieve. Unfortunately, the British Army itself had no suitable cars in Egypt. The Chevrolet dealerships were scoured. This produced 15 vehicles. Harding-Newman persuaded the Egyptian Army to part with another 19. However, this was not the end of it. Cabs were cut off, windscreens were discarded, the springs and chassis were strengthened, gun mountings were installed, and modular ration and fuel cases had to be fitted. Sand tracks had to be obtained and radiators modified with the condensers that Bagnold had developed in the 1920s. This was carried out under the direction of Brigadier Richards at the Ordnance Directorship workshops.

The most crucial need was to recruit and train men for the patrols. Initially a patrol consisted of two officers and around 30 men in 11 trucks, but in due course the patrols were reduced in size to one officer, and 15-18 men in five trucks. As David Lloyd Owen, who joined the LRDG in 1941 and later became its commander remarked, Bagnold would require a very special type of individual in his patrols, who could withstand the obvious problems of hunger, thirst and heat:

He would also require them to tolerate long periods of tedium, just watching and waiting and reporting; at other times they would be expected to work frantically to get some vehicles through the softest patches of sand.

They must be capable of dealing with any unforeseen attack by the enemy on the ground as well as from the air; and they would have to get used to exceedingly uncomfortable travel, lying on top of a lorry laden with petrol, rations, water, ammunition and other hardware. Above all, there was the most tangible strain to which every man would be subjected – the sheer stress of men who would inevitably find themselves for weeks on end behind enemy lines, and liable to be hunted. (Lloyd Owen 1957, 14).

Bagnold said to one recruit (Gordon 1987, 191), "You must forget everything the Army ever taught you and learn to use your initiative".

Wavell and General 'Jumbo' Wilson (figure 49) decided that New Zealanders would be admirable and arranged for Bagnold to meet General 'Tiny' Freyberg (figure 50) who was commanding the New Zealand Division in Cairo. Bernard Freyberg (1889-1963), who was anything but tiny, for a while had practised as a dentist in New Zealand. He was a legendary veteran of the First World War who had earned a Victoria Cross for heroics at the battle of the Somme, DSO and bar, two brevets, had been mentioned in despatches six times and had been often wounded (Connell 1964, 171). Freyberg was involved in the Gallipoli campaign and this very powerfully built man help to carry Rupert Brooke's coffin and dig his grave at Skyros. Freyberg, says Bagnold, "grudgingly agreed to ask for volunteers, provided he could get special permission from his government for its nationals to serve under a foreign commander" (Bagnold 1990, 126). This permission was duly granted and a remarkable number of New Zealand troops volunteered. T patrol was a New Zealand outfit and was very different from G Patrol, which consisted of Guards. They were, in the words of Crichton Stuart, as different as "Guardsman's Blanco from New Zealand butter".

At first sight it appears strange that New Zealanders should have been selected, given that herding sheep on the green pastures of the southern hemisphere archipelago scarcely seems to equip one for daring exploits in a grassless desert in the northern hemisphere. It is perhaps even

Figure 49. 'Jumbo' Wilson.

Figure 50. General 'Tiny' Freyberg VC.

more amazing that in any event they should have proved so adaptable. Bill Kennedy Shaw provides the answer to this paradox:

Most of the first New Zealanders were from the Divisional Cavalry – the 'Div. Cav.' – farmers or the like in civil life, and with a maturity and independence not found in Britishers of similar age. Physically their own fine country had made them on average fitter than us, and they had that inherent superiority which in most of a man's qualities the countryman will always have over the townsman. Many were owner-drivers at home and therefore naturally disposed to take care of their cars; regarding them as a thing to be preserved rather than, as was sometimes the British attitude, as the property of an abstract entity, 'the Government,' whose loss or destruction was small concern of theirs. (Shaw 2000, 19).

To Shaw the New Zealanders always seemed to have a real sense of what the Empire could be to them.

The untravelled Englishman, so long as he gets them, is little interested where his bread and butter comes from. The New Zealander on the contrary has a very real appreciation of where his butter (and mutton) go to. And it is not merely commercially that he sees what the Empire stands for. (Ibid., 19).

Love of the Empire did not, of course, mean that the New Zealanders would love British officers. There would undoubtedly be some misgivings, not least when the officers in question appeared to be beyond the first flush of youth. As Bagnold recalled:

The New Zealanders were surely a little surprised to be met by what must have seemed three quite elderly leaders. I was forty-four, Shaw was the same age but looked older. Clayton was indeed older and had prematurely white hair. However, enthusiasm mounted rapidly when the first of the trucks began to arrive from workshops and they learned what we planned to do and the strange sort of life it would entail. (Bagnold 1990, 126).

They were pleased when they learnt that their army boots were to be discarded for open sandals. There was some opposition to discarding their traditional ANZAC felt hats, but that disappeared on the first outing in the open trucks when the hats all blew off in a cloud. Thereafter they accepted the Arab headdress and even more so after the first strong wind when they found how well it protected their faces from sandblast. For secrecy Bagnold had to get those headdresses from the Palestine police. The sandals were made from a sample of the Indian northwest frontier *chapli* worn by the tribesmen, the only kind of material tough enough to last.

All in all, even though in civilian life or in other army units they may have been immaculate in appearance, members of the LRDG, when on operations, were generally regarded as scruffy. The noted photographer, Cecil Beaton, who knew a thing or two about rough men, remarked in his diaries that:

A more grotesquely assorted, more frightening-looking bunch of bandits it would be hard to imagine. Bearded, covered with dust, with blood-shot eyes, they were less of the world today than like primeval warriors....One apparition with ginger matting for hair, and red eyes staring from a blue-grey dusty face, looked no more human than an ape. (Beaton 1965, 141).

They were, however, disciplined. As Crichton Stuart of the Guards G Patrol put it:

It was no accident that the man whose gun was always ready for action despite the desert dust, the driver whose truck tyres were always at the right pressure, the reliable guard on solitary night watch, was, in barracks, among 'the smartest on the square'. For all that one of the undeniable attractions of the inner desert was the lack, not only of flies, but also of sergeant-majors and generals. (Crichton Stuart 1958, 27).

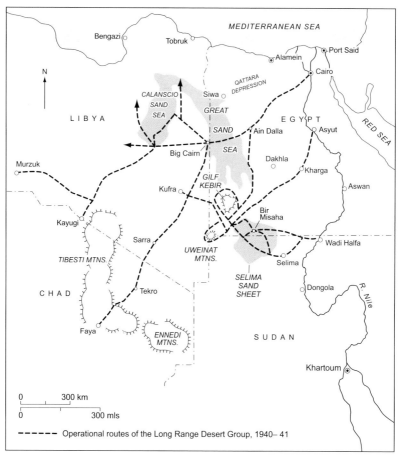

Map 12. LRDG routes 1940-1.

The discipline of the New Zealanders under General Freyberg was different from that of British troops. As Dear and Foot wrote of the General and his men:

He was not a disciplinarian because he considered camaraderie and self-respect were more effective. "You cannot treat a man like a butler," he would say, "and expect him to fight like a lion." Orders were made as suggestions and officers and men were on first-name terms. When Montgomery

Figure 51. An LRDG patrol.

remarked that his troops did not salute much Freyberg replied: "If you wave to them, they'll wave back," and one of his officers said of him, "he's simple as a child and as cunning as a Maori dog". (Dear and Foot 2001, 332).

The first patrol of the Long Range Patrol (LRP) which was soon renamed the Long Range Desert Group or LRDG (map 12) took place in early September 1940. Bagnold took his men to Ain Dalla, site of the start of so much exploration in the 1930s and the gateway to the Great Sand Sea. Bagnold and Shaw demonstrated how to attack the great wall of dunes, and explained the finer points of desert driving, including how to recognise the dangers of liquid sand. After a few days they were ready to cross to the 'Big Cairn' that Clayton had constructed in 1932 on the far side of the Sand Sea (figure 51). From there they would, and did, strike deep into Libya, harassing the Italians both in the north and the south. In addition to the raid on Murzuk described at the start of this volume, the LRDG was involved with the Free French in a raid upon Kufra in eastern Libya. After the death of D'Ornano at Murzuk, the command of the Free French forces in Chad was taken over by Philippe Leclerc de Hauteclocque and he led the attack on Kufra in February 1941. With a force of 101 Europeans and 295 Africans, the French lay siege to the oasis fort, and although they had a rather mixed assortment of trucks, precariously depleted supplies of fuel and food, and limited fire power in comparison with the Italians, they caused the foe to capitulate on 1 March (Kay 1948). Capitano Moreschini's Auto-Saharans fled to the north. The 10-year occupation by the Italians of the oasis, which in April became a major LRDG base, was over. This was important, for as Crichton Stuart remarked (1958, 51), "Whoever ruled Kufra dominated the innermost desert". The LRP's raids were part of what historian Trevor Constable (1999) has called the "Bagnold Bluff." The Bluff was to persuade the Italians, who had huge forces at their disposal in comparison to those available to Wavell, that the British forces were considerably stronger than they in fact were. This would provide time until reinforcements could be assembled. The effect on the Italian command of the patrols and their lightening attacks on distant and isolated places like Murzuk was extraordinary. The bluff was not called:

> The attackers seemed to emerge from the fourth dimension to strike and vanish like lethal ghosts. They appeared, struck and disappeared at widely separate points seemingly within hours of each other. British radio monitors in Cairo and elsewhere intercepted enemy messages of alarm and cries for help pouring into Graziani's headquarters from all over eastern Libya. (Constable 1999, 13).

Graziani's plans for the conquest of Egypt were based on the assumption, backed by intelligence reports, that he faced only weak forces. A rapid victory and occupation of the Nile Delta were anticipated within a few weeks. Yet within a few days of his first battalions crossing into Egypt in September 1940 he began to get disturbing reports of attack – from a direction he believed was completely secure. The British seemed to be everywhere, operating at incredible distances from their base and these assaults gave the war a new dimension. These far-ranging forces might attack his vital rearward lines of communication. Graziani ceased to believe his intelligence reports and their central theme of British weakness. At Sidi Barani on 16 September 1943, in overwhelming strength, the massive Italian army halted its advance. As a report in *The Times* put it:

All the normal enemy desert traffic came to a standstill, all the Italian garrisons were reinforced, and much petrol and oil were expended on a system of land and air patrols, but the Desert Group were never caught. This was a war of nerves with a vengeance, and tales are told of "mysterious noises coming from the desert" which frayed the nerves of Italian commanders and gave garrisons "the jitters". (*The Times*, 14 February 1941, 4).

By February 1941 Wavell's troops had smashed the Italian Army in Cyrenaica. The odious Marshal Graziani pleaded a nervous breakdown, retreated into private life for a time, returning to his military duties only some time later.

The involvement of Bagnold's colleagues from the Zerzura Club dinners of the early 1930s in the LRDG saga is extraordinary. Newbold, then Civil Secretary of the Sudan, arranged diplomatic matters so that Bagnold could link up with Free French forces in Chad. This meant that Murzuk could be attacked. Kennedy Shaw was Intelligence Officer of the LRDG from July 1940 until February 1943. Pat Clayton was wounded and taken prisoner by the Italians on 31 January 1941 in an ambush at Gebel Sherif just south of Kufra, but not before he had been one of the most daring and far-travelled of the team. It was a strange turn of fate that having been spotted by an Italian reconnaissance aircraft, he was ambushed by troops of an Italian Auto-Saharan Company, motorised troops that had so impressed Bagnold a decade or so earlier. Prendergast became commander of the LRDG in August 1941 (when Bagnold himself was promoted to a

Figure 52. LRDG trucks at Siwa.

staff job at GHQ Middle East) and remained officer commanding until
the end of the LRDG's operations in Africa. Rupert Harding-Newman,
who had been on the 1932 Bagnold expedition, was on the operations
staff at Eighth Army and was the link by which Prendergast and Shaw
got their instructions (Lloyd Owen 1957, 57). So, as John Connell
(1964, 244) wrote of Wavell and the LRDG, it was "the first and one of
the most efficient as well as least known of the 'unorthodox' formations
which were inseparably connected with his reputation as a commander"
(figure 52). But, as Connell recognised (Ibid., 245), "the concept was
Bagnold's; the tenacious interest and strong backing were Wavell's".
The LRDG was one of the inspirations for David Stirling's more famous
SAS and often provided a taxi service around the desert for SAS men, as
Virginia Cowles has described in her biography of Stirling, *The Phantom
Major* (1958). The SAS (including George Jellicoe, Sir Stephen Hastings
and Sir Carol Mather) and the LRDG were together involved in some
very daring raids on German airfields and the coast road, Indeed, the SAS
was heavily reliant upon the LRDG, because of their great experience,

their navigational ability, their first-class system of wireless-communications, and their ability to stay in the desert for weeks upon end (figures 53 and 54). Fitzroy Maclean, whose father had been involved with the Light Car Patrols and the capture of Siwa in the First World War, was one of the SAS people who benefited from and admired the LRDG:

> There seemed to be nothing they did not know about the desert….With the help of the sun-compass and the theodolite they had perfected the art of desert navigation and could bring you unerringly to a given hillock or heap of stones hundreds of miles away in the middle of a vast expanse of featureless sand and gravel. They had mapped and charted great stretches of unknown desert and could tell you with unfailing accuracy what to expect in the way of going, where you could hope to get through with a light truck and where with a three-tonner, where to look for cover and how to find the occasional well, half choked up with sand, upon which your survival might depend. They had worked out to the last ounce and the last gallon the amount of food, water and petrol needed to take so many men and so many vehicles for far….Few units could compare with them for morale. (McLean 1949, 206).

The Germans, Italians and Free French never developed anything as good or as innovative as the LRDG and nor for the most part were their vehicles as good. As Andrea Molinari (2007, 11) has remarked, the LRDG was innovative because it did not simply operate from established bases but penetrated deeply into the desert, went well behind enemy lines, and relied on modern means: reliable vehicles, smart equipment, good weaponry and an original approach to desert navigation. In an attempt to emulate this, between summer and autumn 1942, the Italians finally and belatedly set up their own Compagnie Sahariane of motorised, deep-raiding patrols, and their large Autocarro Sahariano AS37s and 42s were effective vehicles. On the other hand, Free French engagements in 1942 consisted of a series of small raids and penetrations that lacked the depth

Figure 53. A Chevrolet truck of the LRDG.

Figure 54. An LRDG truck being extricated from sticky ground.

and freedom of movement that characterised the activities of the LRDG. As for the Germans, according to Molinari (Ibid., 85) they were never capable of producing a vehicle that was really suited to the Western Desert and this was one of the reasons why Almásy's spying expedition used captured British vehicles. It was not simply that they had a desire to deceive the enemy. Remarkably, the Germans never acquired the navigational skills and equipment that were required.

Popski's Private Army

The LRDG was not the only allied special motorised unit to operate during the North African campaigns. There was also Popski's Private Army. Popski was in reality Vladimir Peniakoff (figure 55). When war broke out he sought to join the British Army. There were certain problems in his way. First of all, he was not British. Secondly, he was 42 years old and somewhat portly – he was five foot ten (1.78 m) tall but weighed nearly 15 stone (95 kg). Thirdly, he had been invalided out of the French army in 1919, was short of breath, had high blood pressure and had to be careful with his legs. However, after the German invasion of Belgium in May 1940 he was no longer a mere alien – he was an *allied* alien. So, he approached the British army in Cairo, and after some skill, persistence and slight (but justifiable) deceit he was accepted and commissioned in October 1940. He joined the Eighth Army and was sent into Libya where he led the Libyan Arabs, many of them refugees from the Italian colonial regime. They engaged in spying, sabotage and the rescue of Allied prisoners and stranded airmen. They were taken to and from behind enemy lines by the LRDG. Peniakoff described the routine of an LRDG Patrol:

> Travelling with the LRDG our lives also followed a well-planned pattern: familiar duties left us delightful leisure. On the march, the patrol commander's truck went first, picking the route; then the navigator, then the wireless; the other trucks followed – the fitter came last: his job was to help whoever fell out with mechanical trouble. In the open desert, where there was little risk of detection, we avoided the hazards of travelling in the dark, and journeyed from sunrise to sunset, stopping for an hour or two in the middle of the day for lunch and to allow the wireless operators to get in touch with Headquarters. In single file, a quarter of a mile or so apart, was our usual formation, but we spread out considerably right and left in the areas where we thought enemy planes might be roving. (Peniakoff 1950, 103).

Figure 55. Peniakoff, alias Popski.

When a plane was reported they stopped in their tracks so that their wakes of cloudy dust which made them conspicuous from the air might settle.

The portly Peniakoff was plainly appreciative of the food provided:

> Before starting in the early morning we ate our breakfast of tea, porridge, bacon, biscuit, and jam. Each man's water-bottle was filled for the day and we drove off. Later in the day, when the patrol leader put out a coloured flag, the trucks pulled up and we went to collect our lunch of biscuit, cheese, tinned fish and pickles. Then until the signallers, having completed their job, took down their aerial, we sat on the ground in the shade of our truck and read books, for the heat of the day did not induce talk. (Ibid., 103).

However, things were different at dusk when the trucks came to rest close together and they all went with their mugs for their daily ration of rum and lime-powder. On a fire of dry desert bushes dinner of bully-beef stew and spices was cooked, to be followed by a slice and a half of tinned peach or apricot, and tea. Round the fire they talked and joked till, night drawing on, one after the other they went up to their trucks and laid themselves to sleep on the ground. The signallers went on hammering at their keys long after everyone else was asleep.

In 1942 Peniakoff was authorised to recruit an independent unit initially called the *Number One Long Range Demolition Squadron*. It came to be known as Popski's Private Army. This operated in Libya and Tunisia, employing US Jeeps, and collecting intelligence on enemy troop dispositions and strength, surveying routes, raiding enemy positions behind lines, and generally causing a disproportionate amount of inconvenience to the Axis forces. It seldom had a strength of more than a hundred men. Just how effective it was has been the matter of some speculation. Major General David Lloyd Owen, a commander of the LRDG, was not at all flattering about Popski and argued that Popski's considerable reputation was based more on his strange behaviour than on anything that he ever achieved. Lloyd Owen did not question Popski's personal courage but found he had a muddled mind and was guilty of procrastination, remarking that 'he had become very Arab in his ways, and so he never found it necessary to get a move on or bother about time.' (Lloyd Owen 1980, 96).

Why was this called Popski's Private Army? First, its first official name lacked style and panache. Equally it could hardly be called Peniakoff's Private Army because no one could remember how to spell it or pronounce it. Thus Peniakoff's nickname was employed instead. This was 'Popski' and was the one used by the radiomen at Eighth Army Headquarters. Popski was a hairy little Bolshevik character in a popular British comic strip of the time.

Almásy and the spies

In 1939 Almásy returned to Hungary. He was recruited by the *Abwehr*, the German military intelligence service and was assigned to the German Afrika Korps in 1941. While Bagnold and Peniakoff were operating in the Western Desert, Count Almásy was employing his desert skills working for the Germans (figure 56). He was attached by Rommel to the Brandenburgers, a special intelligence contingent that was the equivalent of the LRDG. In September 1941, Almásy developed a plan to drive 2,700 km via the Jalo Oasis in eastern Libya to the Gilf Kebir and thence to Kharga and Assiut. The reason was to deliver German agents. Two of these were selected. One was Johann Eppler. Born in Alexandria in 1914, his mother was German and his father a German Jew. His mother subsequently married an Egyptian man named Gaafar, who adopted the boy and had him converted to Islam. He was raised in Germany, but returned to Egypt in the 1930s, where he became a merchant apprentice in Cairo. He spoke perfect English and Arabic and looked like an Arab. The other agent was Heinrich Gerd Sandstette, the son of a Professor of Chemistry. Before the war he had spent a good deal of time in Africa and the United States and spoke English well. Almásy used captured British vehicles for this endeavour – three Ford V8 command cars and three Bedford lorries. The journey was named *Operation Salaam*. On 29 April 1942, they set off from Tripoli and less than a month later had reached Assiut on the Nile in middle Egypt. Eppler and Sandstette, of whom Almásy had a rather low opinion, duly made for Cairo, while Almásy returned in his vehicles to Libya. He reported back to Rommel. He was promoted on the spot to Major and was later awarded the Iron Cross, First and Second Class (Kelly 2002, 218). The journey that Almásy took to deliver his two spies, whom he nicknamed Pit and Pan, was a dangerous one. From Tripoli and the Axis base at Jalo (Gialo), the party had to drive through Kufra, which the LRDG used as a major base. They then made for the Gilf

Kebir, where they got lost, and from thence to Kharga. Kharga was a major centre of population, with British police and troops present. British Intelligence followed their route by monitoring their radio signals and decrypting them at Bletchley Park, the British wartime code-breaking establishment.

The two spies established themselves on a houseboat on the Nile, explored the nightspots of Cairo, and made contact with various disaffected elements, including Anwar Sadat, a future President of Egypt. Eppler also seems to have had a liaison with an Egyptian nationalist, Hekmet Fahmy. She was also happened to be a belly dancer who performed at the Kit Kat Cabaret in Cairo. However, their presence was known to British counter-intelligence, and on the night of 24/25 July they were arrested. They spent the rest of the war as POWs.

Almásy was plainly a complex individual. On the one hand he served Rommel in a most distinguished and daring way. On the other hand there is evidence that in the winter of 1944-5, in Budapest, he offered sanctuary, shelter and food to Jews (Almásy 2001, xii). He also counted Jews among his friends, not least his travel companion, Richard Bermann. Eugene Sensenig-Dabbous (2004) makes the point that Almásy was probably not very interested in global politics and that there is very little sign of racist tendencies in his work. Much of what drove him was a profound love of the desert – this probably transcended political matters in his mind. As he wrote in his introduction to *The Unknown Sahara* (1934):

....when I first set foot on the soil of Africa, I became acquainted with the desert, and this first impression was the deepest. Perhaps because driving at full speed into limitless distances is the most perfect expression of total freedom?....I love the endless plain flickering in the reflection of the mirage, the wild, broken rock peaks, the dune belts resembling frozen waves of the ocean. And I love the simple, tough life in the simple camp, both in the

Figure 56. Almásy and spies in the Gilf.

bitterly cold star filled nights and in the scorching sand storms. In the infinity of the desert body, mind and soul are cleansed. Almost invisibly an unshakable belief in a mighty Power above us brings resignation to our humble human existence, even to the extent of offering our life to the desert without a grudge. (Almásy 1934, 6-7).

Curiously, after the war, Almásy was allowed to return to Egypt where King Farouk I, possibly to cock a snook at Great Britain, appointed him as Director of the newly established Desert Institute in Cairo. At its opening in December 1950, he met up with Ralph Bagnold. But very shortly after this Almásy's health deteriorated, and he was flown to Salzburg, where he died of dysentery and a severely diseased liver. He was buried in Austria, where his epitaph includes the title, *Abu Ramla*, father of the sand. A later epitaph on his grave, erected by Hungarian patriots in 1995, honours him as "Pilot, Saharan explorer and discoverer of the Zerzura oasis". His obituary notice in the *Geographical Journal* ended with the judgment that Almásy was "a Nazi but a sportsman." He was certainly a very great explorer.

Epilogue

Although most of the people described in these pages were enthusiastic 'desert-wallopers' (to use a Bagnoldism), this was by no means a universal fetish. The views of some British soldiers emerged in Second World War songs:

It's a man's place in this desert
Where sunshine hurts your eyes.
In fact, I think there's nothing worse
Than the sun, the sand, the flies.

It gets you, does the desert,
It gets you in the end.
You hate and loathe your fellow men.
You quarrel with your friend.

Your water ration seems so small,
The sun your temper tries.
It's an awful place in summer-time
With the sun, the sand, the flies.

The worst part of the desert
Are the sandstorms that abound.
They blow your bloody head off
And knock you to the ground. (Page 1976, 178-80).

British troops, for some reason reserved especial contempt for Mersa Matruh, the coastal settlement where Ball, Jarvis, Boustead and Bagnold served at different times. The reasons for this are not entirely clear, though in the summer, if the *Khamsin* wind blows, whipping up fine white sand, it can become a detestable spot. At other times it was found to be picturesque, and the British, being British, established a pack of hounds there to hunt desert fox. The pack was somewhat motley, consisting of a few real fox hounds, but augmented by native gazelle hounds, called Silugi, several terriers – of sorts – and a few nondescript bedouin pariahs.

The words of several songs about Matruh exist, not all of which are especially tasteful. The least offensive one runs like this:

> We eat the flies, we eat the shit,
> We eat the burning sand.
> Our bones are getting brittle
> And our faces getting tanned.
> Why the hell they keep us here
> We'll never understand
> But we'll sing our blues away.
>
> CHORUS
> *Never, never go to Mersa*
> *Never, never go to Mersa*
> *Never, never go to Mersa*
> *It's a lousy place to stay.* (Page 1976, 52).

It is better perhaps to end with the thoughts of Bill Kennedy Shaw (figure 57), the historian of the LRDG, whose feelings about the desert were remarkably similar to those of Almásy:

> Although in it one saw Nature at her hardest, yet it was a country which many of us, I think, in time began to love. Its attraction for me was that it was so clean. Clean of people, and there are many dirty ones, in every sense of the word, in the Middle East: clean of flies: clean sand instead of clay or limestone dust. Also because it was quiet, at times so silent that you found yourself listening for something to hear. And it was beautiful

Figure 57. Bill Kennedy Shaw (left).

too, not at midday when the hills look flat and lifeless, but in the early morning or late evening when they throw cool, dark shadows and the low sun makes you marvel at the splendid symmetry of the yellow dunes. A psychologist would say, perhaps, that to take pleasure in deserts is a form of escapism, a surrender to the same impulses which made hermits of the early Christians, a refusal to face the unpleasant realities of modern life. He may be right; there are a lot of things in this life worth escaping from…. (Shaw 2000, 31).

The immensity of the Western Desert provided that escape but also produced the setting for some of the most ingenious and intrepid explorations of all time. Was it because so many of the journeys described here were conducted in prosaic motor cars rather than romantically but anachronistically on camels that they have never received the recognition they deserve?

Calendar of Motoring
in the Western Desert, 1916-1942

1916-18	The Light Car Patrols and the Duke of Westminster's armoured cars.
1923-24	Prince Hussein Kemal el Din, Dr John Ball and Major Jarvis to Regenfeld with Citroëns and Fords.
1924	Holland and Bather to edge of Western Desert.
1925	Prince Hussein Kemal el Din and Dr John Ball to Uweinat and Ennedi.
1926	Prince Hussein Kemal el Din to Gilf Kebir and Sarra Well.
1926	Count Almásy and Prince Ezsterházy from Cairo to Khartoum by Steyr.
1926	Court Treatts arrive in Egypt from Cape in their Crossley.
1927	Bagnold's first traverse from Cairo to Siwa.
1927-29	H.J.L. Beadnell and wife on water-drilling duties in the south of Egypt.
1927-30	Mapping of the Qattara Depression by Desert Surveys.
1929	Count Almásy and Prince Ferdinand von Lichtenstein drive from Wadi Halfa to Kharga.
1929	Bagnold explores Great Sand Sea and reaches Ammonite Hill.
1930	Count Almásy operates motor car trials between Wadi Halfa and Uweinat.
1930	Bagnold traverses Great Sand Sea from Ain Dalla, reaches Gilf Kebir, Uweinat and Selima.
1930-1	Patrick Clayton does triangulation from Nile to Uweinat.

1932	Count Almásy and team, including Sir Robert Clayton-East-Clayton, to Gilf Kebir.
1932	Clayton crosses Great Sand Sea east to west and establishes Big Cairn.
1933	Patrick Clayton and Lady Dorothy Clayton to the Great Sand Sea, Kufra and Siwa. Wingate, in search of Zerzura by camel, finds Clayton's car instead.
1933	Count Almásy to Regenfeld and Gilf Kebir.
1933	Clayton to Libyan Desert Glass area and does triangulation through the Great Sand Sea.
1933	Bill Kennedy Shaw and team to Gilf Kebir and El Fasher. Return to Cairo via Great Sand Sea and Siwa.
1935	Count Almásy from Wadi Halfa to Wadi Howar. Explores Great Sand Sea.
1938	Bagnold expedition to Gilf Kebir and Uweinat.
1938	Demarcation of Libyan/Egyptian border in Great Sand Sea.
1940	Formation of LRDG.
1941	The Murzuk raid.
1942	Count Almásy travels with two spies from Libya to Assiut.
1942	'Popski's Private Army' established.

Bibliography

Almásy, L.E. 1930. By motor car from Wadi Halfa to Cairo. *Sudan Notes and Records* 13, 269-278.

Almásy, L.E. 1934. *The Unknown Sahara*. Franklin Tarsulat, Budapest.

Almásy, L.E. 1939. *Unbekannte Sahara*. Brockhaus, Leipzig.

Almásy L.E. 2001. *With Rommel's Army in Libya*. Translated by Andras Zboray, 1st Books Library, Budapest.

Anon 1925. Editorial notes. *Journal of the Royal African Society* 24, 240-253.

Anon 1935. Editorial notes. *Journal of the Royal African Society* 34, 455-462.

Anon 1941. Obituary: Dr John Ball. *Geographical Journal* 98, 301-303.

Anon 1944. Felix Sylvestre Eboué. *Journal of Negro History* 29, 501-503.

Anon 1965, The Qattara Depression, *Geographical Journal* 131, 305.

Asher, M. 1984. *In Search of the Forty Days' Road*. Longman Group, Harlow, Essex.

Atkinson, D. 2003. Geographical knowledge and scientific survey in the construction of Italian Libya. *Modern Italy* 8, 9-29.

Bagnold, R.A. 1931. Journeys in the Libyan Desert 1929 and 1930. *Geographical Journal* 78, 12-39.

Bagnold, R.A. 1933. A further journey through the Libyan Desert. *Geographical Journal* 82, 103-129, 211-235.

Bagnold, R.A. 1935. *Libyan Sands*. Hodder and Stoughton, London.

Bagnold, R.A. 1937. The last of the Zerzura Legend: review. *Geographical Journal* 89, 265-268.

Bagnold, R.A. 1939. An expedition to the Gilf Kebir and 'Uweinat, 1938. *Geographical Journal* 93, 281-313.

Bagnold, R.A. 1941. *Physics of Blown Sand and Desert Dunes*. Methuen, London.

Bagnold, R.A. 1945. Early days of the Long Range Desert Group. *Geographical Journal* 105, 30-46.

Bagnold, R.A. 1966. Obituary: G.W. Murray. *Geographical Journal* 132, 333-334.

Bagnold, R.A. 1990. *Sand, Wind and War. Memoirs of a Desert Explorer.* The University of Arizona Press, Tucson.

Ball, J. 1917. *Desert Reconnaissance by Motor-car. Primarily a handbook for patrol-officers in Western Egypt.* Western Frontier Force. 49pp. MS in Royal Geographical Society.

Ball, J. 1924 Note on the Cartographic Results of Hassanein Bey's Journey, *Geographical Journal* 64, 367-386.

Ball, J. 1927. Problems of the Libyan Desert. *Geographical Journal* 70, 21-38, 105-118, 209-224.

Ball, J. 1928. Remarks on 'lost' oases of the Libyan Desert. *Geographical Journal* 72, 244-258.

Ball, J. 1932. Obituary. Prince Kemal-el-Din Hussein. *Geographical Journal* 80, 367-368.

Beadnell, H.J.L. 1909. *An Egyptian Oasis.* John Murray, London.

Beadnell, H.J.L. 1931. Zerzura. *Geographical Journal* 77, 245-250.

Beaton, C. 1965. *The Years Between: Diaries 1934-44.* Weidenfeld and Nicolson, London.

Belgrave, C.D. 1923. *Siwa: The Oasis of Jupiter Ammon.* John Lane, The Bodley Head, London.

Bermann, R.A. 1934. Historic problems of the Libyan Desert. *Geographical Journal* 83, 456-463.

Bierman, J. 2004. *The Secret Life of László Almásy.* Viking, London.

Bierman, J. and Smith, C. 2002. *Alamein. War without Hate.* Viking, London.

Bimberg, E.L. 2002. *Tricolor Over the Sahara: the Desert Battles of the Free French,* 1940-1942. Greenwood Press, Westport, CT.

Boustead, H. 1971. *The Wind of Morning.* Chatto and Windus, London.

Bubenzer, O. and Riemer, H. 2007. Holocene climatic change and human settlement between the Central Sahara and the Nile Valley: archaeological and geomorphological results. *Geoarchaeology* 22, 607-620.

Carell, P. 1994. *Foxes of the Desert. The Story of the Afrika Korps.* Schiffer Publishing, Atglen, PA.

Clayton, P. 1998. *Desert Explorer.* Zerzura Press, Cargreen, Cornwall.

Connell, J. 1964. *Wavell, Scholar and Soldier.* Collins, London.

Constable, T.J. 1999. Bagnold's Bluff. *The Journal for Historical Review* 18.

Corbyn, E. 1944. Inland from the Eighth Army: the Fighting French in the Libyan Hinterland. *Journal of the Royal African Society* 43, 20-22.

Court Treatt, S. 1927. *Cape to Cairo.* Harrap, London.

Cowles, V. 1958. *The Phantom Major: the Story of David Stirling and the SAS Regiment.* Collins, London.

Crichton Stuart, M. 1958. *G Patrol. The Story of the Guards Patrol of the Long Range Desert Group.* London, Kimber.

Dabous, A.A., and Osmond J.K. 2001. Uranium isotopic study of artesian and pluvial contributions to the Nubian Aquifer, Western Desert, Egypt. *Journal of Hydrology* 243, 242-253.

De Flers, P. and De Flers, P. 2000. *Egypt. Civilization in the Sands.* Konemann, Cologne.

Dear, I.C.B. and Foot, M.R.D. (eds) 2001. *The Oxford Companion to World War II.* Oxford University Press, Oxford.

De Cosson, A. 1935. *Mareotis.* Country Life, London.

Desio, A. 1950. *Le Vie della Sete.* Hoepli, Milan.

Diel, L. 1939. *"Behold our new Empire" – Mussolini.* Hurst and Blackett, London.

Dietzel, M., Kolmer, H., Pölt, P. and Simic, S. 2008. Desert varnish and petroglyphs on sandstone Geochemical composition and climate changes from Pleistocene to Holocene (Libya). *Chemie der Erde* 68, 31-43.

Dun, T.I. 1933. *From Cairo to Siwa across the Libyan Desert with Armoured Cars.* Cairo: Schindler.

Embabi, N. 2004. *The Geomorphology of Egypt, Landforms and Evolution, Volume 1, The Nile Valley and the Western Desert.* The Egyptian Geographical Society, Cairo.

Forbes, R. 1921. *The Secret of the Sahara: Kufara.* Cassell, London.

Forth, N. de R. 1991. *A Fighting Colonel of the Camel Corps. Life Story of Lt Colonel de Lancey Forth DSO (and bar) MC.* Merlin Books, Braunton, Devon.`

Friedman, R. (ed.) 2002. *Egypt and Nubia: Gifts of the Desert.* The British Museum Press, London.

Frischat, G.H., Heide, G., Muller, B. and Weeks, R.A. 2001. Mystery of the Libyan Desert glasses. *Physics and Chemistry of Glasses* 42, 179-183.

Ghoneim, E. and El-Baz, F. 2007. DEM-optical-radar data integration for paleohydrological mapping in the northern Darfur, Sudan: implication for groundwater exploration. *International Journal of Remote Sensing* 28, 5001-5018.

Gilbert, A. 1992. *The Imperial War Museum Book of the Desert War.* BCA, London.

Gooch, J. 2005. Re-conquest and suppression: Fascist Italy's Pacification of Libya and Ethiopia, 1922-1939. *Journal of Strategic Studies* 28, 1005-1032.

Gordon, J.W. 1987. *The Other Desert War. British Special Forces in North Africa, 1940-1943.* Greenwood Press, New York.

Goudie, A.S. 2002. *Great Warm Deserts of the World.* Oxford University Press, Oxford.

Haag, M. 2006. *Introduction*, pp v-xiii in new edition of *The Lost Oases* by A.M. Hassanein Bey. The American University in Cairo Press, Cairo and New York.

Haardt, G.M. and Audouin-Dubreuil, L. 1924. *Across the Sahara by Motor Car: From Touggourt to Timbuctoo.* T. Fisher Unwin, London.

Haggett, P. 1986. Obituary of R.F. Peel. *Transactions of the Institute of British Geographers 11*, 320-372.

Harding King, W.J. 1925. *Mysteries of the Libyan Desert. A Record of Three Years of Exploration in the Heart of that Vast & Waterless Region.* Seeley, Service and Co. Limited, London.

Harding King, W.J. 1928. Lost oases of the Libyan Desert. *Geographical Journal 72*, 244-258.

Harold, J. 2003. Deserts, cars, maps and names. Encountering traces of Claud H. Williams M.C., author of the one hundred and seventy-one page secret *Report on the Military Geography of the North-Western Desert of Egypt.* Paper presented at the ASTENE Conference, Worcester College, Oxford, July 2003.

Hart, B.H.L. (ed.) 1953. *The Rommel Papers.* Collins, London.

Hassanein Bey, A.M. 1924. Crossing the untraversed Libyan Desert. *National Geographic Magazine 46(3).*

Hassanein Bey, A.M. 1925. *The Lost Oases.* Thornton Butterworth, London.

Haynes, C.V. 1989. Bagnold's barchan: a 57-Yr record of dune movement in the Eastern Sahara and implications for dune origin and paleoclimate since Neolithic times. *Quaternary Research 32*, 153-167.

Jarvis, C.S. 1936. *Three Deserts.* John Murray, London.

Jarvis, C.S. 1938. *Desert and Delta.* John Murray, London.

Jarvis, C.S. 1943. *Heresies and Humours.* Country Life Ltd., London.

Jarvis, C.S. 1943. *Half a Life.* John Murray, London.

Jenner, R., List, D. and Badrocke, M. 1999. *The Long Range Desert Group 1940-1945.* Osprey Military, Oxford.

Kádár, L. 1934. A study of the sand sea in the Libyan Desert. *Geographical Journal 83*, 470-478.

Kay, R.L. 1948, Long Range Desert Group in Libya, 1940-41. In *Episodes and Studies*, Volume 1. Wellington: Historical Publications Branch (available at http://www.nzatc.org) (part of the Official History of New Zealand in the Second World War 1939-1945).

Keen, M.J. 1991. Ralph Alger Bagnold. 3 April 1896-28 May 1990. *Biographical Memoirs of Fellows of the Royal Society* 37, 56-68.

Kelly, S. 2002. *The Hunt for Zerzura. The Lost Oasis and the Desert War.* John Murray, London.

Kemal el Din, Prince Hussein 1928. L'exploration du Désert Libyque. *La Géographie* 171-183, 320-336.

Kindermann, K., Bubenzer, O., Nussbaum, S., Riemer, R., Darius, F., Pöllath, N. and Smettan, U. 2006. Palaeoenvironment and Holocene land use of Djara, Western Desert of Egypt. *Quaternary Science Reviews* 25, 1619-1637.

King, W.J.H. 1933, Obituary: Lieut.-Col. Nowell Barnard de Lancey Forth. *Geographical Journal* 81, 479-480.

Kleinmann, B., Horn, P. and Lagenhorst, F. 2001. Evidence for shock metamorphism in sandstones from the Libyan Desert Glass strewn field. *Meteoritics and Planetary Science* 36, 1277-1282.

Kröpelin, S. *et al.* 2008. Climate-driven ecosystem succession in the Sahara: the past 6000 years. *Science* 320, 765-768.

Kuper, R. 2002. Routes and roots in Egypt's Western desert: The Early Holocene Resettlement of the Eastern Sahara. In R. Friedman (ed.), *Egypt and Nubia: Gifts of the desert.* London: British Museum Press, 1-12.

Kuper, R. 2006. After 5000bc: The Libyan desert in transition. *Comptes Rendus Palevol* 5, 409-419.

Lindstädter, J., and Kröpelin, S. 2004. Wadi Bakht revisited: Holocene climate change and prehistoric occupation in the Gilf Kebir Region of the eastern Sahara, SW Egypt. *Geoarchaeology* 19, 753-778.

Lloyd Owen, D. 1957. *The Desert my Dwelling Place.* Cassell, London.

Lloyd Owen, D. 1980. *Providence Their Guide. The Long Range Desert Group 1940-1945.* Harrap, London.

Lodge, J. 2005. Re-conquest and Suppression: Fascist Italy's Pacification of Libya and Ethiopia, 1922-39. *The Journal of Strategic Studies* 28, 1005-1032.

Maclean, F. 1949. *Eastern Approaches.* London: Jonathan Cape and the Book Society.

Mason, M. 1936. *The Paradise of Fools.* London: Hodder and Stoughton.

Massey, W.T. 1918. *The Desert Campaigns.* London: Constable.

Maxwell, T.A. and Haynes, C.V. 2001. Sand sheet dynamics and Quaternary landscape evolution of the Selima Sand Sheet, southern Egypt. *Quaternary Science Reviews* 20, 1623-1647.

McGuirk, R. 2007. *The Sanusi's Little War.* London: Arabian Publishing.

McHugh, W.P. 1975. Some archaeological results from the Bagnold-Mond Expedition to the Gilf Kebir and Gebel Uweinat, southern Libyan Desert. *Journal of Near Eastern Studies* 34, 31-62.

McHugh, W.P., Breed C.S., Schaber G.G., McCaulcy, J.F., and Szabo, B.J. 1988, Acheulian sites along the 'Radar Rivers', Southern Egyptian Sahara. *Journal of Field Archaeology* 15, 361-379.

Molinari, A. 2007. *Desert Raiders: Axis and Allied Special Forces 1940-43.* Oxford: Osprey Publishing.

Monod, T. and Diemer, E. 2000. *Zerzura: L'Oasis Légendaire du Désert Libyque.* Editions Vents de Sable, Paris.

Morgan, M. 2000. *Sting of the Scorpion: the Inside Story of the Long Range Desert Group.* Sutton Publishing, Stroud.

Murray, G.W. (ed.) 1950. *The Survey of Egypt, 1898-1948.* Paper No. 50. Survey Dept, Cairo.

Murray, G.W. 1960. Obituary: Wilfrid Jennings Bramly, MBE, MC. *Geographical Journal* 126, 258-9.

Murray, G.W. 1967. *Dare me to the Desert.* George Allen and Unwin, London.

Ness, P. 1929. *Two Thousand Miles on Two Continents.* Methuen, London.

Newbold, D. 1928. More lost oases of the Libyan Desert. *Geographical Journal* 72, 547-554.

Nicoll, K. 2001. Radiocarbon chronologies for prehistoric human occupation and hydroclimatic change in Egypt and Northern Sudan. *Geoarchaeology: An International Journal* 16, 47-64.

Nöther, W. 2003. *Die Erschliessung der Sahara durch Motorfahrzeuge 1901-1936*. Belleville, Munich.

O'Carroll, B. 2003. *Bearded Brigands: the diaries of Trooper Frank Jopling*. Leo Cooper, Barnsley.

Ondaatje, M. 1992. *The English Patient*. Bloomsbury, London.

Page, M. 1976. *For Gawdsake Don't Take Me*. Hart Davis MacGibbon, London.

Paillou, P. *et al.* 2006. An extended field of crater-shaped structures in the Gilf Kebir region, Egypt: Observations and hypotheses about their origin. *Journal of African Earth Sciences* 46, 281-299.

Parker, J. 2004. *Desert Rats*. Headline, London.

Peel, R.F. 1939 Rock-paintings from the Libyan Desert. *Antiquity* 13, 389-402.

Peel, R.F. 1941. Denudational landforms of the Central Libyan Desert. *Journal of Geomorphology* 3, 3-23.

Peel, R.F. 1942. The Tibu peoples and the Libyan Desert. *Geographical Journal* 100, 73-87.

Penderel, H.W.G.J. 1934. The Gilf Kebir. *Geographical Journal* 83, 449-470.

Peniakoff, V. 1950. *Popski's Private Army*. Jonathan Cape, London.

Pitt, B. 1980. *The Crucible of War. Wavell's Command*. Jonathan Cape, London.

Reclus, E. 1871. *The Earth*. Chapman and Hall, London.

Ridley, G. 1985. *Bend'Or Duke of Westminster*. Robin Clark Limited, London.

Robinson, C.A., Werwer, A., El-Baz, F., El-Shazly, M., Fritch, T. and Kusky, T. 2007. The Nubian aquifer in southwest Egypt. *Hydrogeology Journal* 15, 33-45.

Rolls, S.C. 1937. *Steel Chariots in the Desert*. Jonathan Cape, London.

Sebba, A. 1988. *Enid Bagnold.* George Weidenfeld and Nicholson, London.

Sandford, K.S. 1940. Libyan frontiers. *Geographical Journal* 96, 377-388.

Sandford, K.S. 1944. Obituary: Hugh John Llewellyn Beadnell. *Geographical Journal* 103, 86-87.

Sensenig-Dabbous, E. 2004. Will the real Almásy please stand up! Transporting Central European Orientalism via The English Patient. *Comparative Studies of South Asia, Africa and the Middle East,* 24, 163-179.

Shaw, W.B.K. 1929. Darb el Arba'in. The Forty Days' Road. *Sudan Notes and Records* 12, 63-71.

Shaw, W.B.K. 1934. The Mountain of Uweinat. *Antiquity* 8, 63-72.

Shaw, W.B.K. 1936. An expedition to the southern Libyan Desert. *Geographical Journal* 87, 193-221.

Shaw, W.B.K. 1943. Desert navigation: some experiences of the Long Range Desert Group. *Geographical Journal* 102, 253-258.

Shaw, W.B.K. 1945. *Long Range Desert Group.* Collins, London.

Shaw, W.B.K. 2000. *Long Range Desert Group.* Greenhill Books, London.

Somerville, M. 1858. *Physical Geography*, 4th edition. John Murray, London.

Swinson, A. 1969. *The Raiders: Desert Strike Force.* Macdonald, London.

Sykes, C. 1959. *Orde Wingate.* Collins, London.

Thesiger, W. 1987. *The Life of My Choice.* Collins, London.

Tiltman, M.H. 1935. *Women in Modern Adventure.* Harrap, London.

Underwood, J.R. and Giegengack, R.F. 2002. Piracy on the high desert: the Long-Range Desert group 1940-1943. In P. Doyle and M.R. Bennett (eds.) *Fields of Battle: Terrain in Military History.* Kluwer, Dordrecht, 311-324.

Vivian, C. 2000. *The Western Desert of Egypt.* The American University in Cairo Press, Cairo.

von der Esch, H. 1944. *Weenak – die Karavane Ruft.* Brockhaus, Leipzig.

Wellard, J. 1964. *The Great Sahara.* Hutchinson, London.

Williams, C.H. 1919. *Report on the Military Geography of the North-Western Desert of Egypt.* War Office Handbook.

Williams, C.H. undated. *Light Car Patrols in the Libyan Desert.* 85pp manuscript in the Royal Geographical Society.

Wilson, Field-Marshal Lord. 1950. *Eight Years Overseas. 1939-1947.* Hutchinson, London.

Windmill, L.A. 2005. *A British Achilles, the Story of George, 2nd Earl Jellicoe.* Pen and Sword Military, Barnsley.

Wingate, O. 1934. In search of Zerzura. *Geographical Journal* 83, 281-308.

Wright, J.W. 1945. War-time exploration with the Sudan Defence Force in the Libyan Desert, 1941-43. *Geographical Journal* 105, 100-111.

Wynter, H.W. 2001. *Special Forces in the Desert War, 1940-1943.* Public Record Office, Kew.

Yunnie, P. 2002. *Fighting with Popski's Private Army.* Greenhill Books, London.

Sources of pictures

(ASG = author's own photograph)

1. Office of War Information Photograph Collection, Library of Congress.
2. By kind permission of the Royal Geographical Society.
3. ASG.
4. By kind permission of NASA.
5. By kind permission of NASA.
6. ASG.
7. By kind permission of NASA.
8. Top: ASG; bottom: courtesy NASA.
9. By kind permission of NASA.
10. RAF official photograph.
11. ASG.
12. ASG.
13. Hassanein Bey, A.M. 1925, *The Lost Oases*, 82
14. ASG. Cover of *The English in Egypt with the Life of General Gordon and other Pioneers of Freedom*, London, James Sangster (Anon., no date).
15. Nöther, W. 2003, *Die Erschliessung der Sahara durch Motorfahrzeuge 1901-1936*. Belleville, Munich, fig. 13.
16. Nöther, W. 2003, *Die Erschliessung der Sahara durch Motorfahrzeuge 1901-1936*. Belleville, Munich, fig. 24.
17. Nöther, W. 2003, *Die Erschliessung der Sahara durch Motorfahrzeuge 1901-1936*. Belleville, Munich, fig. 23.
18. By kind permission of C.H. Williams's family.
19. By kind permission of the Royal Geographical Society.
20. http://www.firstworldwar.com/photos/graphics/ gw_westminister_01.jpg. Accessed 21/10/08.

21. ASG.

22. Ridley, G. 1985, *Bend D'Or Duke of Westminster.*

23. Forbes, R. 1921, *The Secret of the Sahara, Kufara,* 2.

24. By kind permission of Andras Zboray.

25. By kind permission of the Royal Geographical Society.

26. Jarvis, C.S. 1943, *Half a Life,* 80.

27. RGS collection, by kind permission of the Royal Geographical Society.

28. Clayton, P. 1998, *Desert Explorer,* Plate 24, 102, with kind permission of the author.

29. Clayton, P. 1998, *Desert Explorer,* Plate 5, 21, with kind permission of the author.

30. Clayton, P. 1998, *Desert Explorer,* Plate 13, 54, with kind permission of the author.

31. Court Treatt, S. 1927, *Cape to Cairo,* Frontispiece.

32. Sykes, C. 1959, *Orde Wingate,* 385.

33. Lloyd Owen, D. 2000, *Providence their Guide,* plate 2.

34. By kind permission of the Royal Geographical Society.

35. By kind permission of the Royal Geographical Society.

36. ASG, taken in the Imperial War Museum, London.

37. Boustead, H. 2002 *The Wind of Morning,* Plate 16, by kind permission of Linden Publishing and Mrs A.L. West.

38. Nöther, W. 2003, *Die Erschliessung der Sahara durch Motorfahrzeuge 1901-1936.* Belleville, fig. 146.

39. Kelly, S. 2002, *The Hunt for Zerzura,* Plate 13.

40. Tiltman, M.H. 1935, *Women in Modern Adventure,* 234 with the permission of Chambers Harrap Publishers, Edinburgh.

41. Proceedings British Academy, 1986, in http://www.proc.britac. ac.uk/tfiles//71p523.pdf. Accessed 19/02/07.

42. Mason, M. 1936, *The Paradise of Fools,* 209.

43. Mason, M. 1936, *The Paradise of Fools,* frontispiece.

44. Kelly, S. 2002, *The Hunt for Zerzura,* Plate 5.

45. Kennedy Shaw, W.B. 1945, *Long Range Desert Group*, 101.
46. http://afrika-korps.de/forum/. Accessed 19/4/07.
47. Diel, L. 1939, *"Behold our New Empire" – Mussolini*, 220.
48. ASG: taken at the Imperial War Museum.
49. Wilson, Lord 1950, *Eight Years Overseas*, frontispiece.
50. Wilson, Lord 1950, *Eight Years Overseas*, 352.
51. By kind permission of the Imperial War Museum.
52. By kind permission of the Imperial War Museum.
53. By kind permission of the Imperial War Museum.
54. By kind permission of the Imperial War Museum.
55. Peniakoff, V. 1950, *Popski's Private Army*, 210, Cassell Plc., a division of the Orion Publishing Group.
56. http://www/fjexpeditions.com/desert/history/expeditions/sal4.jpg Accessed 19/02/07. Kindly provided by Michael Rolke and with the permission of Herr Otokar Seubert.
57. Lloyd Owen, D. 2000, *Providence Their Guide*, Plate 4.

INDEX

(references to maps shown in brackets)